SpringerBriefs in Computer Science

Series editors

T0171961

SpringerBriefs present concise summaries of cutting-edge research and practical applications across a wide spectrum of fields. Featuring compact volumes of 50 to 125 pages, the series covers a range of content from professional to academic.

Typical topics might include:

- A timely report of state-of-the art analytical techniques
- A bridge between new research results, as published in journal articles, and a contextual literature review
- A snapshot of a hot or emerging topic
- An in-depth case study or clinical example
- A presentation of core concepts that students must understand in order to make independent contributions

Briefs allow authors to present their ideas and readers to absorb them with minimal time investment. Briefs will be published as part of Springer's eBook collection, with millions of users worldwide. In addition, Briefs will be available for individual print and electronic purchase. Briefs are characterized by fast, global electronic dissemination, standard publishing contracts, easy-to-use manuscript preparation and formatting guidelines, and expedited production schedules. We aim for publication 8–12 weeks after acceptance. Both solicited and unsolicited manuscripts are considered for publication in this series.

More information about this series at http://www.springer.com/series/10028

Alvin Penner

Fitting Splines to a Parametric Function

Springer

Alvin Penner
FONTHILL
ON, Canada

ISSN 2191-5768   ISSN 2191-5776 (electronic)
SpringerBriefs in Computer Science
ISBN 978-3-030-12550-9   ISBN 978-3-030-12551-6 (eBook)
https://doi.org/10.1007/978-3-030-12551-6

Library of Congress Control Number: 2019931899

This Springer imprint is published by the registered company Springer Nature Switzerland AG.
The registered company address is: Gewerbestrasse 11, 6330 Cham, Switzerland

to Nina
for being willing to listen

Preface

This work began as an attempt to see whether it was possible to fit a spline curve to another parametric function in such a way that the spline curve would respond smoothly and continuously to changes in the shape of the parametric function. In other words, would the resulting fitted curve be suitable for use in an animation? Since then, the scope of the project has changed somewhat to include an investigation of the intersections that occur between three different areas of study that normally would not touch each other: least squares orthogonal distance fitting (ODF), spline theory, and topology. The ODF method has become the standard technique used to develop mathematical models of the physical shapes of objects, due to the fact that it produces a fitted result that is invariant with respect to the size and orientation of the object. It is typically applied in cases where there are thousands of discrete measurements available on the physical shape of an object. In this case, there are two implicit assumptions that are being made: namely, that we are interested only in one solution (the one that has the minimum error) and that we are unable to substantially change the shape of the object being fit. We will relax these two assumptions by fitting splines to a family of parametric functions whose shape can be continuously modified. In this way, we can investigate the response of the spline curve to changes in the shape of the curve we are trying to fit. The quality of this response may be particularly important in cases where one wishes to produce a smooth animation of the motion of an object. If the response is discontinuous, the quality of the animation will suffer as a result. During these exercises, it became increasingly clear that there are often a number of solutions that can exist and that the interaction between them is important. Different solutions can spontaneously coalesce and disappear, and it is sometimes necessary to arbitrarily switch from one to another in order to minimize the error. Therefore, it is not sufficient to focus only on the minimum error solution since the definition of this solution will change as the object's shape changes.

The second area of study that will be touched on is the theory of splines. We have used six different splines to fit the shape of a simple family of epitrochoid curves: two types of Bézier curve, two uniform B-splines, and two Beta-splines. In theoretical studies of these splines, the emphasis is usually on how to develop mathematical shapes in such a way that they can be usefully implemented by a designer, such as a draftsman operating CAD software. In other words, the emphasis is on developing user-friendly ways of manipulating these shapes in a way that is mathematically complete and consistent. For example, in the development of the theory of Beta-splines, new degrees of freedom have been introduced and have been associated with such concepts as *tension* and *bias* in order to make them accessible to the designer. We will borrow these results *as is* but will make a slight digression to apply them to a least squares optimization problem. In the case of Beta-splines, this is challenging and, to the best of our knowledge, has not been done before, due to nonlinear couplings that exist between the different adjustable parameters in the spline model.

The final area of interest is topology. There are often multiple solutions to the ODF method, and these solutions can always be classified as being either local minima or saddle points of different degree. We classify them according to their *Morse index*, which counts the number of negative eigenvalues of the second-order response matrix. Since there are many solutions, two topological questions immediately arise: are there rules that can be applied concerning the relative number of local minima and saddle points, and are there different mechanisms available by which solutions can either merge and disappear or cross over each other and interchange roles? We will propose some simple rules which can be used to determine if a given set of solutions is internally consistent in the sense that it has the appropriate number of each type of solution. The rule that relates the number of occurrences of each type can be viewed as an instance of *Euler's characteristic* equation for polyhedra. We will also observe experimentally two distinct mechanisms by which solutions can either merge or cross each other. The merge of solutions is an instance of a *fold catastrophe*, while the crossover of solutions does not appear to have any analog in *catastrophe theory*. A diagnostic test will be developed to allow us to easily determine which type of event is occurring.

The organization of the work is as follows. Chapter 2 presents a general derivation of the ODF method, customized for fitting a continuous parametric function. This contains some results which may be new or at least expressed in unfamiliar form. Chapter 3 summarizes some previously derived properties of splines. We have included only those results that are absolutely essential for the description of a uniform B-spline. The results of the ODF curve fit using two types of Bézier curve are given in Chaps. 4 and 8; two types of uniform B-spline fits are described in Chaps. 6 and 7; and Chaps. 9 and 10 present the Beta-spline curve fits. The cubic Bézier curve fit in Chap. 4 presents some interesting topological problems, so Chap. 5 represents a digression to discuss the process of how solutions coalesce and/or cross each other. Other than that, the chapters are ordered roughly according to the degree of computational difficulty of the fit, with the cubic Bézier being the easiest and the Beta1-spline the most difficult.

The original purpose of the study was to see if the fitted spline shapes would respond smoothly to changes in the shape of the curve we are fitting. This is of some importance when discussing the animation of shapes. In general, the answer to this question is "no," but it is hoped that the results may be helpful in determining which particular type of spline would be most useful in any case. In some cases, it may be desirable to use the spline curve that presents the least computational challenges, such as a uniform B-spline, and in other cases, there may be symmetry considerations that would justify the use of a more complex spline such as the Beta2-spline. In either case, one must be aware of the topological changes that can occur as the shape of the object changes.

It is a pleasure to acknowledge the inspiration provided by the developers of Inkscape, which stimulated the initial work in this area.

The ODF calculations were performed using the Java code at the repository: https://github.com/alvinpenner/Spiro2SVG/

Fonthill, ON, Canada   Alvin Penner
September 2018

Contents

Chapter 1
Introduction

When creating images suitable for use in vector graphics it is necessary at some point to approximate complex shapes with simpler shapes which are more easily rendered on the computer. When doing so, one typically uses the least squares fitting error as the criterion by which to judge the quality of the conversion. However, if the purpose of the conversion is to produce an animated sequence of images, then one might also be concerned with whether the various parameters in the fitted curve are changing smoothly as the original shape changes. It would not be desirable to have an animation that appeared to be jerky as a result of discontinuous changes in fitted parameters.

To investigate the question of smoothness of response, a family of hypoTrochoid curves was created which can morph continuously from an extreme where there is zero curvature at one endpoint, due to a double inflection point, to an intermediate shape which is an arc of a circle, to a final shape where the zero curvature is at the other endpoint, so that there has been a complete reversal of the roles of the start point and the end point. The Least Squares Orthogonal Distance Fitting method was used to fit this family of curves using a variety of spline curves of differing complexity. The purpose of the fit was to see if the error in the curve fit would vary continuously as the shape changed, and to see if the individual spline parameters would also vary continuously. The splines were chosen to be either cubic (5 cases) or quartic (1 case), and fall into the general categories of being either Bézier, uniform B-spline, or Beta-spline. An attempt was made to evaluate the relative merits of the various types of spline with respect to ease of implementation and quality of fit. The details of the spline curves are summarized in Table 1.1.

While evaluating the results it was found that sometimes a large number of solutions were possible, so it was necessary to develop some rules to test whether the set of solutions obtained was internally consistent. It was also found to be helpful to classify solutions as being either local minima or saddle points, according to their

© The Author(s), under exclusive license to Springer Nature Switzerland AG 2019
A. Penner, *Fitting Splines to a Parametric Function*,
SpringerBriefs in Computer Science, https://doi.org/10.1007/978-3-030-12551-6_1

Table 1.1 List of spline properties

Chapter	Name	Degree	Bézier segments	Control points	Deg. of freedom
4	Cubic Bézier	3	1	4	2
6	B-spline5	3	2	5	4
7	B-spline6	3	3	6	6
8	Quartic Bézier	4	1	5	4
9	Beta2-spline	3	2	5	5
10	Beta1-spline	3	2	5	5

Morse index. Finally, as the shape of the fitted object changes, there are two distinct ways in which the topology of the solution space can change, due to solutions that coalesce and disappear, or in some cases cross each other and change shape as they do so. A diagnostic method for distinguishing between these cases is described.

Chapter 2
Least Squares Orthogonal Distance Fitting

In the last 25 years the subject of Least Squares Orthogonal Distance Regression [3, 10] or Orthogonal Distance Fitting (ODF) [1, 4, 7] has received a lot of attention. This seems to be motivated primarily by a desire to produce a fitted result that is independent of the location and orientation of the object being fitted. It is made practically possible by the increased availability of fast computers and numerically robust algorithms [8] for performing the calculations. Historically, regression models would normally assume that the direction of movement due to experimental error was known a priori to be either vertical or horizontal; or perhaps specified externally by some kind of independent measure of experimental error [5]. The ODF method removes this restriction by minimizing the distance from the measured point to the curve, so that each individual data point can have a unique direction of movement to reach the curve we are using for the fit. The typical application of the ODF method is to use various types of spline curves to fit a set of discrete experimental measurements of an object's shape, but we will use it instead to fit a smooth parametric function. We are specifically interested in the question of how the fit responds to incremental changes in the shape of the curve to be fit, and also the related questions of how many solutions exist for any specific shape, and how their character changes when they either coalesce or cross over each other. Since the optimization problem is non-linear, the answers to these questions are not known ahead of time.

2.1 Definition of Error Function

We begin by defining what we mean by residual error in the fit. Define $\mathbf{f}(\mathbf{a}, u) = (f_x, f_y)$ as the two-dimensional, piecewise-continuous, spline we are adjusting to perform the fit, while $\mathbf{g}(t) = (g_x, g_y)$ is the curve to be fit. In other treatments [1], $\mathbf{g}(t)$ would be a discrete set of experimental data points, but in our case both $\mathbf{f}(\mathbf{a}, u)$ and $\mathbf{g}(t)$ are parametric functions. The parametric variable for $\mathbf{g}$ is $t \in [t_1, t_2]$, while $\mathbf{f}$ has the parametric variable $u \in [0, m]$ for a spline with m segments, $m - 1$ splices. In the notation of Ref. [1, p. 55], $u(t)$ is called a "location parameter", while $\mathbf{a} = \{a_i\}_{i=1}^n$ is a set of "model parameters" which can be adjusted to improve the fit. These will typically be coordinates of control points. For each t we define the residual error as

$$\|\mathbf{f}(\mathbf{a}, u) - \mathbf{g}(t)\| \triangleq \sqrt{(f_x(u) - g_x(t))^2 + (f_y(u) - g_y(t))^2}$$

where $u(t)$ will be chosen so as to minimize this distance. Performing a derivative of residual error with respect to u, we obtain the constraint

$$(f_x(u) - g_x(t))f_x'(u) + (f_y(u) - g_y(t))f_y'(u) = 0 \qquad (2.1)$$

where $f_x'(u) \triangleq \partial f_x / \partial u$. In effect, this equation states that the residual error vector, $\mathbf{f}(\mathbf{a}, u) - \mathbf{g}(t)$ will be perpendicular to the curve $\mathbf{f}(\mathbf{a}, u)$. This equation will normally not be solvable analytically (for a cubic Bézier curve $\mathbf{f}$, Eq. (2.1) is quintic in u), so we will solve it numerically using the Newton-Raphson method [6]. We will require u in (2.1) to converge to within a tolerance of 10^{-9} before terminating the calculation. In practice, when calculating $u(t)$, we subdivide the range of $t \in [t_1, t_2]$ into N equal segments and calculate u only at these points, using the result from the previous t value to initialize the next calculation. Given a definition of residual error we now define the overall error functional as

$$F(\mathbf{a}, u) = \frac{1}{2} \int_{t_1}^{t_2} [(f_x(u) - g_x(t))^2 + (f_y(u) - g_y(t))^2] dt$$

where it is implicitly assumed that $u(t)$ has been calculated using (2.1), and we will perform the integration numerically by dividing the range of t into N (= 100) segments and using the trapezoidal rule. We then define the root-mean-square (rms) error to be $\sqrt{2F/(t_2 - t_1)}$. The task now is to find extrema of F with respect to $\mathbf{a}$, subject to the constraint that (2.1) is satisfied at all times. We will refer to these as critical points [2], meaning that the gradient of F is zero with respect to $\mathbf{a}$.

2.2   Character of Solution

Before attempting the optimization, we introduce some matrix notation, along with a brief description of how the solutions to this problem can be qualitatively characterized. We wish to approximate F, at any given value of $\mathbf{a}$, as a locally quadratic function of $\mathbf{a}$, so we can calculate its maximum/minimum. We do so with the Taylor expansion

$$F = F_0 + \mathbf{L}^t \mathbf{a} + \frac{1}{2}\mathbf{a}^t \mathbf{Ma}$$

where $\mathbf{a}^t = (a_1, \ldots, a_n)$, $\mathbf{L}^t = (L_1, \ldots, L_n)$, $L_i = dF/da_i$, and $\mathbf{M} = \{d^2 F/da_i da_j\}_{i,j=1}^n$. The gradient vector $\mathbf{L}$ and the second-order response matrix $\mathbf{M}$ will be calculated below, where it will also be seen that $\mathbf{M}$ is symmetric. For now we note, formally, that the local extremum of F will occur when $\mathbf{a}$ is the solution of the equation $\mathbf{Ma}_0 = -\mathbf{L}$. Expanding about this point we express F in the simpler form:

$$F = F_0 - \frac{1}{2}\mathbf{a}_0^t \mathbf{Ma}_0 + \frac{1}{2}(\mathbf{a} - \mathbf{a}_0)^t \mathbf{M}(\mathbf{a} - \mathbf{a}_0).$$

This makes it clear that the response of F will be purely quadratic when we are located at the critical point $\mathbf{a}_0$. Now note that $\mathbf{M}$ can be diagonalized by a unitary transform $\mathbf{U}$ such that $\mathbf{U}^t \mathbf{MU} = \mathbf{D}$ (diagonal), and that the eigenvalues will be real since $\mathbf{M}$ is symmetric. Define a transformed set of shape parameters $\mathbf{a}' = \mathbf{U}^t(\mathbf{a} - \mathbf{a}_0)$ and re-express F as:

$$F = F_0 - \frac{1}{2}\mathbf{a}_0^t \mathbf{Ma}_0 + \frac{1}{2}\sum_{i=1}^n \lambda_i (a_i')^2$$

where λ_i are the eigenvalues of $\mathbf{M}$. Since the different modes of response of the function F do not interact with each other in any way, we can now make some qualitative statements about the nature of the critical point $\mathbf{a}_0$. We do so using the Morse index [2, p. 55], which counts the number of negative eigenvalues of $\mathbf{M}$. If all the eigenvalues are positive (index = 0) then we have a local minimum; if there is a single negative eigenvalue (index = 1) we have a saddle point solution. We will find below that saddle point solutions are fairly common and will often coalesce with local minima and disappear as we modify the shape of the curve $\mathbf{g}(t)$. Similarly, if the Morse index = 2, we will refer to this as a double saddle point. These are somewhat rare, and when they occur it is likely that they will eventually coalesce with a single saddle point and disappear as we change the shape of $\mathbf{g}(t)$. The form of the disappearance, when plotted against a parameter that controls the shape of $\mathbf{g}(t)$, will be qualitatively comparable to the figure in Ref. [2, p. 63], showing solutions that merge and annihilate each other in pairs.

2.3 Optimization of $F(\mathbf{a}, u)$

The optimization of F with respect to $\mathbf{a}$ is made non-trivial by the dependence on $u(t)$. In effect we have two sub-problems which are coupled to each other: optimization of $u(t)$ and optimization of F with respect to $\mathbf{a}$, which depends on u. There are at least three types of solution method available. The first is simultaneous optimization of all variables, called the "total method" [1, p. 25 (Algorithm I)]. The second is to formally solve the equations for $\mathbf{a}$ (which may sometimes be linear) and then embed that solution into the calculation of an optimum set of $u(t)$, which are called "nodes" in Ref. [4, p. 276]. The third method is to solve for $u(t)$ first, using (2.1), and then use a Newton-Raphson type of iteration to update $\mathbf{a}$. This is called the "variable-separation" method [1]. We will implement this method using a coordinate-based performance index similar to Algorithm III (FhG) [1, p. 67]. This method involves alternating back and forth between an inner loop which calculates $u(t)$ and an outer loop which calculates $\mathbf{a}$, until both converge. The inner loop has already been defined in (2.1); the outer loop requires the evaluation of $\mathbf{L}$ and $\mathbf{M}$. Evaluating these terms is complicated by the implicit dependence of F on u, so that the operator d/da_i becomes $\partial/\partial a_i + (\partial u/\partial a_i)\partial/\partial u$. We begin by evaluating $\mathbf{L}$:

$$L_i \triangleq dF/da_i = \int_{t_1}^{t_2}(f_x(u) - g_x(t))(\partial f_x/\partial a_i + f_x'(u)\partial u/\partial a_i)dt$$

$$+ \int_{t_1}^{t_2}(f_y(u) - g_y(t))(\partial f_y/\partial a_i + f_y'(u)\partial u/\partial a_i)dt$$

(2.2)

Evaluating this term requires the knowledge of $\partial u/\partial a_i$, which can be obtained by differentiating (2.1), to get:

$$0 = (\partial f_x(u)/\partial a_i + f_x'(u)\partial u/\partial a_i)f_x'(u) + (\partial f_y(u)/\partial a_i + f_y'(u)\partial u/\partial a_i)f_y'(u)$$

$$+ (f_x(u) - g_x(t))(\partial f_x'(u)/\partial a_i + f_x''(u)\partial u/\partial a_i)$$

$$+ (f_y(u) - g_y(t))(\partial f_y'(u)/\partial a_i + f_y''(u)\partial u/\partial a_i)$$

This can be written in the simpler form:

$$E(u)\partial u/\partial a_i = - f_x'(u)\partial f_x(u)/\partial a_i - (f_x(u) - g_x(t))\partial f_x'(u)/\partial a_i$$

$$- f_y'(u)\partial f_y(u)/\partial a_i - (f_y(u) - g_y(t))\partial f_y'(u)/\partial a_i$$

(2.3)

where

$$E(u) = f_x'(u)f_x'(u) + f_x''(u)(f_x(u) - g_x(t))$$

$$+ f_y'(u)f_y'(u) + f_y''(u)(f_y(u) - g_y(t))$$

(2.4)

Note that $E(u)$ is not dependent on the index i, which will be helpful later (2.8). It is perhaps worthwhile to note the role that $\partial u/\partial a_i$ plays in the previous literature. In Ref. [1, p. 65], using Algorithm II (distance-based performance index), this term does not seem to be present. In Ref. [1, p. 68], using Algorithm III (coordinate-based performance index), the term is present in [1, Fig. 4.5], but it is not clear how important it is. We will derive explicit expressions for the contribution of this term below, so that it is possible to evaluate its importance.

The evaluation of the response matrix $\mathbf{M}$ proceeds by differentiating (2.2) to get:

$$M_{ij} \triangleq d^2 F/da_i da_j = \int_{t_1}^{t_2} G_{ij}(\mathbf{a}, u)dt \qquad (2.5)$$

where

$$
\begin{aligned}
G_{ij} = {} & (\partial f_x/\partial a_i + f_x'(u)\partial u/\partial a_i)(\partial f_x/\partial a_j + f_x'(u)\partial u/\partial a_j) \\
& + (f_x(u) - g_x(t)) \left[\begin{array}{l} \partial^2 f_x/\partial a_i \partial a_j + \partial f_x'/\partial a_i(\partial u/\partial a_j) \\ +(\partial f_x'/\partial a_j + f_x''(u)\partial u/\partial a_j)\partial u/\partial a_i \\ +f_x'(u)\partial^2 u/\partial a_i \partial a_j \end{array} \right] \\
& + (\partial f_y/\partial a_i + f_y'(u)\partial u/\partial a_i)(\partial f_y/\partial a_j + f_y'(u)\partial u/\partial a_j) \\
& + (f_y(u) - g_y(t)) \left[\begin{array}{l} \partial^2 f_y/\partial a_i \partial a_j + \partial f_y'/\partial a_i(\partial u/\partial a_j) \\ +(\partial f_y'/\partial a_j + f_y''(u)\partial u/\partial a_j)\partial u/\partial a_i \\ +f_y'(u)\partial^2 u/\partial a_i \partial a_j \end{array} \right]
\end{aligned} \qquad (2.6)
$$

This equation shows explicitly that $\mathbf{M}$ is symmetric, as expected. Up to now we have not made use of the properties of $u(t)$, namely that it yields a minimum distance to $\mathbf{g}(t)$. We do so now, by substituting (2.1) into (2.2) to find that the term proportional to $\partial u/\partial a_i$ has a coefficient of zero, which yields the simpler result:

$$L_i = \int_{t_1}^{t_2} [(f_x(u) - g_x(t))\partial f_x/\partial a_i + (f_y(u) - g_y(t))\partial f_y/\partial a_i]dt \qquad (2.7)$$

Similarly, if we substitute (2.1) into (2.6), we find that the term proportional to $\partial^2 u/\partial a_i \partial a_j$ disappears as well, to yield

$$
\begin{aligned}
G_{ij} = {} & \partial f_x/\partial a_i(\partial f_x/\partial a_j) + (f_x(u) - g_x(t))\partial^2 f_x/\partial a_i \partial a_j \\
& + [f_x'(u)\partial f_x/\partial a_j + (f_x(u) - g_x(t))\partial f_x'/\partial a_j]\partial u/\partial a_i \\
& + [f_x'(u)\partial f_x/\partial a_i + (f_x(u) - g_x(t))\partial f_x'/\partial a_i]\partial u/\partial a_j \\
& + [f_x'(u)f_x'(u) + (f_x(u) - g_x(t))f_x''(u)]\partial u/\partial a_i(\partial u/\partial a_j) \\
& + \partial f_y/\partial a_i(\partial f_y/\partial a_j) + (f_y(u) - g_y(t))\partial^2 f_y/\partial a_i \partial a_j \\
& + [f_y'(u)\partial f_y/\partial a_j + (f_y(u) - g_y(t))\partial f_y'/\partial a_j]\partial u/\partial a_i \\
& + [f_y'(u)\partial f_y/\partial a_i + (f_y(u) - g_y(t))\partial f_y'/\partial a_i]\partial u/\partial a_j \\
& + [f_y'(u)f_y'(u) + (f_y(u) - g_y(t))f_y''(u)]\partial u/\partial a_i(\partial u/\partial a_j)
\end{aligned}
$$

This last result is particularly helpful because the term $\partial^2 u/\partial a_i \partial a_j$ would have been challenging to calculate. In this last expression we have chosen to arrange the terms of G_{ij} according to their dependence on $\partial u/\partial a_i$. Now note that the coefficients of $\partial u/\partial a_i$ are identical to the right hand sides of either (2.3) or (2.4). Substituting these equations into the expression for G_{ij} we obtain the simpler result:

$$
\begin{aligned}
G_{ij} = {} & \partial f_x/\partial a_i(\partial f_x/\partial a_j) + (f_x(u) - g_x(t))\partial^2 f_x/\partial a_i \partial a_j \\
& + \partial f_y/\partial a_i(\partial f_y/\partial a_j) + (f_y(u) - g_y(t))\partial^2 f_y/\partial a_i \partial a_j \\
& - E(u)\partial u/\partial a_i(\partial u/\partial a_j)
\end{aligned}
\tag{2.8}
$$

This is the final expression for G_{ij}, suitable for calculating M_{ij}. We note in passing that it could have been derived somewhat more simply by explicitly imposing (2.1) at all stages of the derivation; specifically, before we took the derivative of (2.2) to produce (2.6). However, this would have hidden the process by which the term $\partial^2 u/\partial a_i \partial a_j$ cancels, which is helpful to know. It also would have potentially hidden the impact that (2.1) has on the propagation of numerical error in the iteration process when the determinant of $\mathbf{M}$ is small (Fig. 2.3). However, in future derivations of the response of the solution to external changes (Chap. 5) we will explicitly assume this constraint is satisfied at all times.

The expression (2.8) for G_{ij} contains three distinct types of contributions. The first type is proportional to $\partial f_x/\partial a_i(\partial f_x/\partial a_j)$ and the corresponding term in y. If we were solving a problem with discrete data points $\mathbf{g}(t)$, this type of term would be represented by the expression $\mathbf{J}^t \mathbf{J}$ where $\mathbf{J}$ is a Jacobian matrix [3, p. 340]. The second type is proportional to $\partial^2 f_x/\partial a_i \partial a_j$ and the corresponding term in y. This would be represented by a Hessian matrix in a discrete formulation [3, p. 340]. This type of term would be ignored if we were implementing the Gauss-Newton approximation method, which is fairly common [1, p. 28]. In our case we cannot ignore this term because we wish to calculate $\mathbf{M}$ exactly so that we can attribute significance to the eigenvalues as alluded to above. However, it should be noted that for a B-spline curve with no constraints on the control point positions, this term will be zero in any event because the dependence on $\mathbf{a}$ is linear. It is only in the presence of internal constraints on the control points, such as appear in Beta-splines (Chaps. 9 and 10), that this term becomes significant. The final type of contribution is proportional to $\partial u/\partial a_i(\partial u/\partial a_j)$. This term arises because any adjustment of $\mathbf{a}$ will cause a simultaneous response in u if we impose (2.1). It is not immediately clear how important this term will be in general: however, a numerical example is shown in Fig. 2.1. This is from a curve fit of a cubic Bézier with two degrees of freedom to a hypoTrochoid curve with $c = 10$ (Chap. 4). We have shown the contributions of the $\mathbf{J}^t \mathbf{J}$ term (solid) and the $\partial u/\partial a_i(\partial u/\partial a_j)$ term (dotted) to the matrix elements G_{11}, G_{12}, and G_{22} plotted as a function of t. The actual matrix element G_{ij} will be the difference between these two curves. We see that there is a very high level of cancellation between the two terms, so the contribution of $\partial u/\partial a_i(\partial u/\partial a_j)$ can definitely not be ignored.

Fig. 2.1 Two contributions to $G_{ij}(t)$

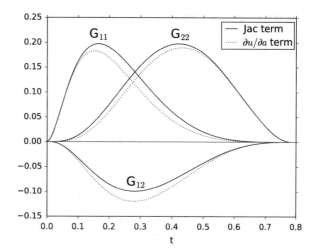

We now use Newton's method to search for the optimum value of **a**. Given that we have calculated **L** and **M** at an estimated a_0, and that we have expressed dF/da as $L + M(a - a_0)$ in a local region around a_0, we set $dF/da = 0$ by solving

$$M(a - a_0) = -L. \tag{2.9}$$

We will solve this matrix equation for $a - a_0$ using the Gauss-Jordan elimination method with full pivoting: routine "gaussj" in Ref. [9, p. 39]. This method was chosen in order to minimize error propagation in cases where the determinant of **M** is small. With this new estimate of **a**, we recalculate $u(t)$ using (2.1) and then repeat the sequence until both $u(t)$ and **a** converge. We require all the elements of **a** to converge to within a tolerance of 10^{-9} before terminating the calculation. It is worthwhile to note the effect that the terms in $\partial u/\partial a_i (\partial u/\partial a_j)$ have in (2.9). Since they reduce the size of G_{ij}, they will also reduce **M** as well, which will increase the gain in (2.9) when we calculate $\Delta a = a - a_0$. This will speed up the convergence rate significantly.

Some comments on numerical performance: we will normally start the calculation by using a simpler fitting method to initialize the current one. For example, when performing a fit using a single-segment cubic Bézier curve, start by first fitting the curvature at the endpoints (Sect. 4.2) to get a preliminary value of **a**. Similarly, when using a multiple-segment B-spline curve, start by fitting a single-segment Bézier curve and re-expressing it as a B-spline. Failing that, use a previous curve fit at a slightly different shape of $g(t)$ to initialize the fit for the current shape. The convergence rate will typically be linear at the end of the iteration, but will be slower at the start. There may be cases where the method fails to converge. Typically this will happen when one of the **a** parameters becomes physically unrealistic, like a negative Bézier control arm length, or a case where $u(t)$ has multiple solutions. We reject all cases where the relationship between u and t is not a one-to-one

Fig. 2.2 Convergence of $\Delta\mathbf{a}$ and Δrms error for a cubic Bézier

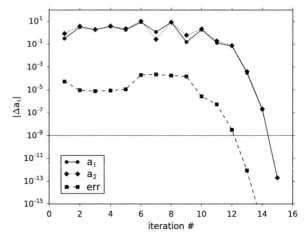

Fig. 2.3 Convergence of $\Delta\mathbf{a}$ for a Beta2-spline

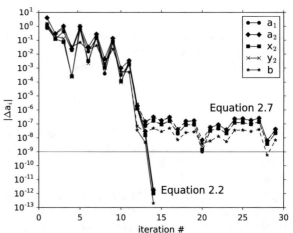

relationship. An example of "typical" convergence behavior is shown in Fig. 2.2. This is from a fit of a cubic Bézier (Chap. 4), with two degrees of freedom, to a hypoTrochoid curve ($c = 6, a_1 = 27.0$ in Fig. 4.3) for a solution that is a saddle point. Figure 2.2 shows $\log|\Delta a_i|$ and $\log|\Delta$rms error| for 16 iterations. The convergence rate is initially very slow for about 10 iterations and then improves considerably as we approach the converged result.

We can also encounter convergence problems when two solutions coalesce and disappear, or when multiple solutions are close together. This will normally be associated with a near-zero determinant of the matrix $\mathbf{M}$, which means the gain in the calculation of $\Delta\mathbf{a}$ will be large. Figure 2.3 shows the convergence behavior of a Beta2-spline (Chap. 9) fitting the hypoTrochoid curve ($c = 2, a_1 = 35.38$ in Fig. 9.2) for a solution that is a saddle point. This particular point is also relatively close to a point of coalescence of solutions. The figure shows the default behavior obtained when (2.7) is used to evaluate $\mathbf{L}$, which in turn determines the response $\Delta\mathbf{a}$.

The iteration initially appears to be converging normally, but then degenerates into what looks like random variation, and fails to achieve the desired precision of 10^{-9}. If we persist for a few hundred iterations the calculation will eventually achieve the desired precision, but this will happen as a result of what appears to be pure chance rather than systematic convergence. A much better behavior is obtained if we evaluate $\mathbf{L}$ using (2.2), which was the original definition. This behavior is plotted as a solid line in Fig. 2.3 and it converges normally, in 14 iterations, similar to Fig. 2.2. The difference between the two methods is that (2.7) assumes implicitly that $u(t)$ in (2.1) has been calculated precisely, while (2.2) does not make this assumption. As a result, (2.7) appears to be highly susceptible to random error in $u(t)$ while (2.2) is not. A side note on error tolerance is perhaps in order: the iteration method consists of two nested loops. The inner loop is the calculation of $u(t)$, which has its' own unique error tolerance in (2.1). The outer loop is the calculation of $\mathbf{a}$, which has a separate error tolerance in (2.9). In (2.9) the inner loop error (which shows up in $\mathbf{L}$), will get transformed into outer loop error (in the variable $\mathbf{a}$) through the matrix $\mathbf{M}^{-1}$, which is the reason why a small determinant causes convergence problems. To solve the particular convergence problem in Fig. 2.3, an attempt was made to reduce the error in $u(t)$ by tightening the inner loop tolerance. However this was not very successful, for reasons that are not well understood. An alternative solution would be to loosen the tolerance in the outer loop, since Fig. 2.3 makes it clear that we are almost on the verge of achieving the desired precision of 10^{-9}. However, this does not address the fundamental question: which is, why the error is being propagated in the first place. In our calculations we chose instead to use (2.2) whenever it was necessary. In the large majority of cases the two methods are indistinguishable, as they are in Fig. 2.2, but in some special cases (2.2) was able to restore normal convergence behavior to an otherwise ill-conditioned problem.

References

1. S.J. Ahn, *Least Squares Orthogonal Distance Fitting of Curves and Surfaces in Space*. LNCS, vol. 3151 (Springer, Berlin, 2004)
2. J.-P. Aubin, I. Ekeland, *Applied Nonlinear Analysis* (Dover, New York, 2006)
3. A. Björck, *Numerical Methods for Least Squares Problems* (SIAM, Philadelphia, 1996)
4. C.F. Borges, T.A. Pastva, Total least squares fitting of Bézier and B-Spline curves to ordered data. Comput. Aided Geom. Des. **19**, 275–289 (2002)
5. W.E. Deming, *Statistical Adjustment of Data* (Dover, New York, 1964)
6. C.-E. Fröberg, *Introduction to Numerical Analysis*, 2nd edn. (Addison-Wesley, Reading, 1969)
7. Y. Liu, W. Wang, A revisit to least squares orthogonal distance fitting of parametric curves and surfaces, in *Advances in Geometric Modeling and Processing*. LNCS, vol. 4975 (Springer, Berlin, 2008)
8. D.W. Marquardt, An algorithm for least-squares estimation of nonlinear parameters. J. Soc. Indust. Appl. Math. **11**(2), 431–441 (1963)
9. W.H. Press, S.A. Teukolsky, W.T. Vetterling, B.P. Flannery, *Numerical Recipes in C*, 2nd edn. (Cambridge University Press, New Delhi, 1993)
10. D.A. Turner, *The Approximation of Cartesian Coordinate Data by Parametric Orthogonal Distance Regression*. Ph.D. Thesis, University of Huddersfield, UK (1999)

Chapter 3
General Properties of Splines

In this section we summarize some of the properties of B-splines [1, 3, 4, 5, 6], to be applied in more detail later. The discussion will focus on the purely functional aspects of the various components, as opposed to a mathematical description. We will not attempt to describe the more general class of NURBS (non-uniform rational B-splines) because there is no support for such curves in the standard graphics API of most computers, unless one uses specialized software such as Autocad.

A B-spline is defined to be a piecewise continuous parametric function given by [5, Eq. 2.2]:

$$\mathbf{f}(u) = \sum_{i=0}^{n} N_{ip}(u)\mathbf{P}_i \tag{3.1}$$

where, at any given u, we will always have $\sum_{i=0}^{n} N_{ip}(u) = 1$. The shape of the spline is manipulated using a set of control points $\{\mathbf{P}_i\}_{i=0}^{n}$ which in our case are two-dimensional. The functions $N_{ip}(u)$ are called basis functions. They are piecewise continuous functions, and determine the behavior of the spline within each continuous segment, as well as the behavior at the joins between segments. They are functions of the parametric variable u, of degree p, order $(p + 1)$. In the special case where the spline consists of only one continuous segment, we call it a Bézier curve, and the basis functions $N_{ip}(u)$ become Bernstein polynomials [5, Eq. 1.8]:

$$B_{ip}(u) = \frac{p!}{i!(p-i)!}u^i (1-u)^{p-i} \tag{3.2}$$

where it is assumed in this case that $u \in [0, 1]$. In the general case, the range of u will be divided into multiple segments and the behavior at the joins between them will be determined by a knot vector $U = \{u_i\}_{i=0}^{m}$. The knot values u_i are not necessarily unique; there may be duplicates. The subset of knot values that

© The Author(s), under exclusive license to Springer Nature Switzerland AG 2019
A. Penner, *Fitting Splines to a Parametric Function*,
SpringerBriefs in Computer Science, https://doi.org/10.1007/978-3-030-12551-6_3

are unique are called breakpoints [5, p. 47]. The purpose of the knot vector is twofold: we can to some extent modify the shape of the spline by adjusting the distance between breakpoints u_i, and we can modify the degree of continuity at each breakpoint by adjusting the degree of multiplicity of the u_i at the breakpoint. With respect to the spacing between u_i we will always assume a constant spacing in this discussion, so we will restrict ourselves to what are called "uniform" B-splines. With respect to multiplicity, we allow for the possibility that there may be more than one u_i that have the same value. If so, then each new u_i that has the same value as a previous one will represent the loss of one degree of continuity of the curve. For example, if we have a curve of degree n, the continuity will be C^n in the absence of a breakpoint and will decrease by one at the position u_i whenever we introduce a new knot at this numerical value. By C^n continuity we mean that both $d^n f_x(u)/du^n$ and $d^n f_y(u)/du^n$ are continuous. A few examples may illustrate this: a cubic Bézier is represented by the knot vector $U = (0\,0\,0\,0\,1\,1\,1\,1)$. Since there are no u_i in the internal region between 0 and 1, the curve consists of a single segment which is cubic. At the endpoints $u = 0$ and $u = 1$ the function is discontinuous since we began with C^3 continuity and lost 4 degrees of continuity due to the u_i. Incidentally, this also has the consequence that the function $\mathbf{f}(0)$ will be identical to the control point $\mathbf{P}_0$, and $\mathbf{f}(1)$ will equal the control point $\mathbf{P}_n$. (Normally, this would not be the case at a breakpoint.) We will restrict ourselves to B-splines of this type, which are called "clamped" [1, p 408]. A second example is given by the knot vector $U = (0\,0\,0\,0\,1\,2\,2\,2\,2)$ applied to a cubic spline. This consists of two segments which are both cubic but which have C^2 continuity at $u = 1$. Similarly, the knot vector $(0\,0\,0\,1\,1\,2\,2\,2)$ applied to a quadratic spline would yield a "clamped" quadratic spline with two segments and a cusp at $u = 1$, since $\mathbf{f}(1)$ is continuous but $\mathbf{f}'(1)$ is not. The purpose of augmenting the knot vector in this way is to introduce new degrees of freedom: each new knot in U will introduce a new control point $\mathbf{P}_i$, which can be adjusted at will without modifying the degree of continuity at the breakpoint. That is to say, the continuity at the breakpoint is controlled by U, not by the value of $\mathbf{P}_i$. Finally, we will use the convention here that each segment of U will be given a length of 1, so that N segments will have a length N. The scaling of U is not important since both (3.3) and (3.4) are dimensionless in the sense that the breakpoints u_i are present in both numerator and denominator. However, it is important that the full range of U must be scanned when evaluating the curve: when comparing two curves for the purposes of knot insertion, or decomposition into Bézier segments, we will require them to share the same range of U.

   Given the knot vector U we can now calculate the $N_{ip}(u)$ quite generally using a recurrence relation [5, Eq. 2.5]:

$$N_{i,0}(u) = \begin{cases} 1 \text{ if } u_i \leq u < u_{i+1} \\ 0 \text{ otherwise} \end{cases}$$

(3.3)

$$N_{i,p}(u) = \frac{u - u_i}{u_{i+p} - u_i} N_{i,p-1}(u) + \frac{u_{i+p+1} - u}{u_{i+p+1} - u_{i+1}} N_{i+1,p-1}(u)$$

For a B-spline of degree p we would begin by calculating all the N_{i0}. This yields a set of step functions which are defined on the various $[u_i, u_{i+1})$ intervals. Then proceed to the calculation of the set N_{i1}, which will be linear functions defined on the same set of intervals. The recursion stops when we finish the sequence N_{ip}, which will be functions of degree p. A number of concrete examples are given in Ref. [5]. As can be seen, the calculations are extremely tedious and can be quite lengthy as well. However, the advantage of this method is that these basis functions need be evaluated only once and can then be used with any set of control points with the guarantee that the desired continuity at the breakpoints will always be automatically maintained. The control points used here represent a minimal data set which is necessary to achieve the desired continuity. The alternative would involve breaking up the individual segments into separate Bézier curves which would lead to a much larger set of independent variables, where we would have to artificially impose internal constraints on the Bézier control points to maintain the desired continuity. (This is a situation that we will have to deal with later when we discuss Beta-splines.)

Given the basis functions N_{ip} we could, in principle, proceed to the optimization of the ODF curve fit. However, there are a number of practical problems that are still unresolved: namely, how to initialize the spline at the start of the ODF optimization, how to render it without actually writing explicit code to do so when we are finished, and how to determine the number of required control points. We begin by answering these questions for a cubic Bézier curve. A cubic Bézier can be fit to another curve quite well by either fitting the slope and curvature at the endpoints, or by fitting some other property like the center of mass. This can be used as an initial estimate for the ODF calculation (Chap. 4). The cubic Bézier can also be rendered directly by calling on standard graphics API libraries [2] without the need for writing low-level rendering code. As for control points, the number of control points is equal to the order (degree + 1) since there is only one segment [3, p. 213]. This allows us to complete an ODF calculation using a cubic Bézier. Now we wish to use this information to initialize a more complex B-spline calculation. In other words, we wish to recast a cubic Bézier in the form of a more complex B-spline without changing its shape. To do this we use a technique known as "knot insertion". The purpose of knot insertion is to deliberately downgrade the degree of continuity at a specific u_i value by inserting a new knot value, in return for which we gain a new degree of freedom in the form of a control point. The basis functions N_{ip} will be modified according to (3.3). The relationship between the new set of control points, $\mathbf{Q}$, and the old set, $\mathbf{P}$, is given by [5, Eq. 5.11]

$$\mathbf{Q}_i = \alpha_i \mathbf{P}_i + (1 - \alpha_i)\mathbf{P}_{i-1} \qquad (3.4)$$

where

$$\alpha_i = \begin{cases} 1 & \text{for } i \le k - p \\[2mm] \dfrac{\bar{u} - u_i}{u_{i+p} - u_i} & \text{for } k - p + 1 \le i \le k \\[2mm] 0 & \text{for } i \ge k + 1 \end{cases}$$

and where $\bar{u}$ is the new knot. Implementing this algorithm for $\mathbf{Q}_i$ is considerably easier than calculating the basis functions $N_{ip}(u)$. When we perform this knot insertion the curve does not initially change its shape in any way; however, it has the potential to do so in the future, since it is now expressed as a member of a larger class of basis functions. We can now use this new representation of the curve as an initial estimate in the ODF calculation and can proceed with the optimization of the new class. Once this is done, we wish to render the final result by re-expressing the optimized curve as a sequence of cubic Béziers, if possible. We do so by considering each knot position separately, and inserting knots until each breakpoint has a multiplicity equal to the order of the curve (degree + 1). This works well for all the splines we are considering here, which are all piecewise cubic splines, except for the quartic Bézier (Chap. 8) which cannot be simplified in this way.

Finally, we note that the number of control points will satisfy the equation [4, p. 111] and [6, p. 68]:

$$knots = control points + degree + 1$$

where *knots* includes all multiple knots. This is true quite generally for any open (non-periodic) spline, even for those cases where the endpoints are not clamped.

A brief note on the number of degrees of freedom (d.f.) present in the B-spline representation, compared to an equivalent sequence of Béziers spliced together. If we have a cubic B-spline with 5 control points, knot vector U = (0 0 0 0 1 2 2 2 2), the total number of degrees of freedom is 10. This can also be expressed as two separate cubic Bézier curves where each segment has 4 control points, for a total of 16 degrees of freedom, compared to 10 for the B-spline. The difference becomes more pronounced as we impose endpoint conditions. We will typically force the endpoints to be fixed, as well as the slope (dy/dx) at the endpoints, which removes 6 degrees of freedom from both fits. The comparison is now 10 d.f. for the Bézier representation versus 4 d.f. for the B-spline, which gives some indication of the efficiency of the B-spline representation. Admittedly, some of these additional d.f. in the Bézier representation are trivial to resolve, such as forcing the endpoint of one Bézier to be equal to the start point of the next. However, some of the internal constraints on the Bézier representation will be non-trivial, if they involve the curvature at the breakpoint. For this reason the B-spline representation is always preferred if it is available, because it is the most efficient way of achieving, and maintaining, the desired level of continuity.

In the following chapters we will evaluate six different types of splines as they are fit to a family of curves: two Bézier curves, two uniform B-splines, and two Beta-splines. (The Beta-splines are B-spline curves in which we have modified the continuity constraints to allow them to satisfy what is known as *second degree geometric continuity* [3, p. 294], which is less restrictive than C^2 continuity. As a result they can have either one or two new degrees of freedom while maintaining the same visual appearance at breakpoints.) We will qualitatively compare them in three areas, namely rms error, ability to respond smoothly to changes in the shape of the curve to be fit, and complexity of the set of solutions.

References

1. M.K. Agoston, *Computer Graphics and Geometric Modeling* (Springer, London, 2005)
2. D. Appleman, *Visual Basic Programmer's Guide to the Win32 API* (Ziff-Davis Press, Emeryville, 1996)
3. R.H. Bartels, J.C. Beatty, B.A. Barsky, *An Introduction to Splines for Use in Computer Graphics & Geometric Modeling* (Morgan Kaufmann, Los Altos, 1987)
4. S. Biswas, B.C. Lovell, *Bézier and Splines in Image Processing and Machine Vision* (Springer, London, 2008)
5. L. Piegl, W. Tiller, *The NURBS Book* (Springer, Berlin, 1995)
6. H. Prautzsch, W. Boehm, M. Paluszny, *Bézier and B-Spline Techniques* (Springer, Berlin, 2002)

Chapter 4
ODF Using a Cubic Bézier

The simplest spline we will use to perform the ODF fit is a cubic Bézier. Figure 4.1 shows the construction of this curve [2, p. 337]. The curve passes through the endpoints at P_0 and P_3. The control points at P_1 and P_2 determine the shape, but the curve does not pass through them. At each endpoint, the curve will be tangent to the corresponding control arm, either the vector $P_1 - P_0$ or the vector $P_2 - P_3$. The control arms have length a_1 and a_2, which are arbitrarily defined to be positive when the two control arms are pointing inwards, towards each other. The lengths of the control arms will roughly control the curvature: normally a shorter arm length will correspond to higher curvature. The parametric equation for the curve is (3.1) using Bernstein polynomials (3.2), where $P_i = (x_i, y_i)$ and $u \in [0, 1]$. When fitting the Bézier curve to another curve, we will match the two endpoints and the slopes at the endpoints. This leaves only two unknown parameters, a_1 and a_2. In Fig. 4.1 the angles θ_1 and θ_2 are defined to be perpendicular to the velocity vector. We anticipate the length a_2 to be positive so define this length to be positive in the direction opposite to the velocity at P_3. The control points can now be re-expressed as:

$$
\begin{aligned}
P_1 &= (x_1, y_1) = (x_0 - a_1 \sin\theta_1, \ y_0 + a_1 \cos\theta_1) \\
P_2 &= (x_2, y_2) = (x_3 + a_2 \sin\theta_2, \ y_3 - a_2 \cos\theta_2).
\end{aligned}
\tag{4.1}
$$

This allows a distinction between those variables already known ($P_0, P_3, \theta_1, \theta_2$) and those as yet unknown (a_1, a_2). The unknown a_i will be determined using the ODF method.

© The Author(s), under exclusive license to Springer Nature Switzerland AG 2019
A. Penner, *Fitting Splines to a Parametric Function*,
SpringerBriefs in Computer Science, https://doi.org/10.1007/978-3-030-12551-6_4

Fig. 4.1 Cubic Bézier
construction

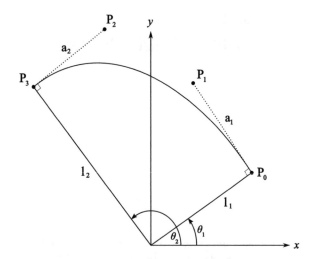

4.1   Fitting a Function with a Double Inflection Point

So far we have described the general fitting method, ODF, and the spline functions
we are using to perform the fit. Now we describe the function to be fit. This is
actually a family of functions called hypoTrochoids. These have been made popular
by the child's game called Spirograph. The curves are interesting because they can
be smoothly morphed from one extreme type of behavior to another, allowing us to
test the ability of our curve-fitting method to respond smoothly to these changes.
There are two specific types of behavior we wish to investigate. First, there is the
transition from a symmetric shape to an asymmetric shape, where by asymmetric we
mean simply a large difference in the curvature at the endpoints. Secondly, there is
the transition from an endpoint behavior which can be reasonably well approximated
as being quadratic, to one which is primarily quartic, due to a double inflection point.
This will test the ability of a cubic spline to emulate behavior which is not cubic in
nature.

We wish to fit a hypoTrochoid [3], defined by:

$$\mathbf{g}(t) = ((a - b)\cos t + c\cos((1 - a/b)t), (a - b)\sin t + c\sin((1 - a/b)t))$$

This is the shape drawn by a pen located a distance c away from the center of a wheel
(called a rotor) of radius b rolling on the inside of another wheel (called a stator) of
radius a. We will choose the specific values $a = 240$, $b = 60$, and will allow c to vary
between -20 and 20. This object has four-fold rotational symmetry and it also has
a mirror symmetry about an axis tilted at 45°. Figure 4.2 shows the curve at various
c values, for $t \in (0, \pi/4)$. Note that there is a complementary property in these
shapes: if we tilt the axis by 22.5°, then the curve at $-c$ is the mirror image of the
curve at c. Therefore the Bézier arm lengths will obey the relation $a_2(c) = a_1(-c)$.
The curve at $c = 0$ is a circular arc. We have chosen $c = \pm 20$ as a limit because

Fig. 4.2 hypoTrochoid
curves

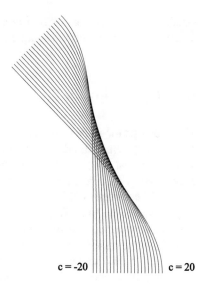

c = -20   c = 20

in this case the curve has a double inflection point at one endpoint, by which we
mean that two normal inflection points have coalesced into one. By varying c we
can observe a smooth transition from a case where we have zero curvature at the
start point, to a symmetric circular case, and then to the complementary case of zero
curvature at the end point.

4.2 Initializing a Cubic Bézier

We begin the ODF calculation by initializing the Bézier curve to fit the hypoTrochoid curvature at the endpoints. The local curvature of a parametric curve is defined
[1, p. 37] as $\kappa = |d\mathbf{T}/ds|$ where $\mathbf{T}$ is the unit tangent vector and s is arc length:

$$\kappa = (x'y'' - y'x'')/((x')^2 + (y')^2)^{3/2} \tag{4.2}$$

where $x' = dx/du$. Evaluating the curvature at the endpoints in terms of the
variables a_1 and a_2 yields the constraints:

$$-(y_3 - y_0 - a_2 \cos\theta_2)\sin\theta_1 - (x_3 - x_0 + a_2 \sin\theta_2)\cos\theta_1 = 3a_1^2\kappa(0)/2 \tag{4.3}$$

$$(y_3 - y_0 - a_1 \cos\theta_1)\sin\theta_2 + (x_3 - x_0 + a_1 \sin\theta_1)\cos\theta_2 = 3a_2^2\kappa(1)/2 \tag{4.4}$$

where $\kappa(0)$ and $\kappa(1)$ will be evaluated using the hypoTrochoid curve. Since (4.3)
is linear in a_2, we can solve it for a_2 and substitute that expression into (4.4) to

obtain a quartic equation for a_1. This can be solved analytically. Of the four possible solutions, we use only those solutions with positive a_1 and a_2.

4.3 Optimizing the Fit

Each iteration for a new **a** consists of first calculating $u(t_i)$ at N values of t_i using the Newton-Raphson method. We use $u(t_i)$ to initialize the calculation of $u(t_{i+1})$, and use the fact that $u(t_1) = 0$ since the endpoints of the two curves are forced to agree. From this $u(t)$ profile we calculate the rms error, and then update **a**. We use (3.1) and (3.2) to evaluate $\partial^n \mathbf{f}/\partial u^n$ and (4.1) to evaluate $\partial \mathbf{f}/\partial a_i$. From this we calculate $\partial u/\partial a_i$ and **L** and **M** (2.3), (2.7), (2.8). We note that the Hessian terms $\partial^2 \mathbf{f}/\partial a_i \partial a_j$ are zero for this spline, as they will be for all cases except the Beta-splines. The new model parameters **a** are calculated from (2.9) and typically converge in a few dozen iterations. Initializing the calculation by fitting curvature at the endpoints is a good start point in most cases, but sometimes it is more convenient to just use the most recent converged result at a nearby value of the shape parameter c, the hypoTrochoid pen distance.

Figure 4.3 shows the Bézier arm lengths a_1 obtained from the curvature fit and the ODF method. We have plotted only a_1, since $a_2(c) = a_1(-c)$. The figure shows two qualitatively different types of solution that intersect each other. There is an S-shaped solution produced by both the curvature and ODF methods. Then there is a solution that has the form of a closed oval shape, more or less centered around $c = 0$, which was not predicted by the curvature fit. For the moment we will discuss only the S-shaped solution. At $c = 20$ the length a_1 is relatively small because the curvature at the start point is high. Then, at $c = 0$, we have three acceptable solutions, one with $a_1 = a_2$ and two asymmetric solutions; and at $c = -20$

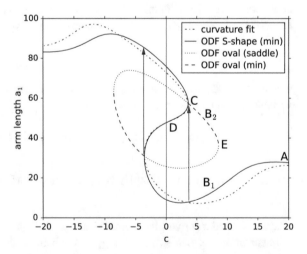

Fig. 4.3 Cubic Bézier arm length a_1

Fig. 4.4 Cubic Bézier rms
error

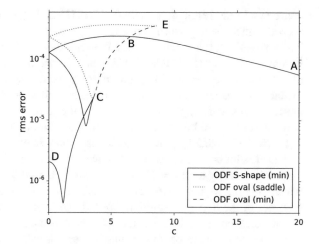

we find a_1 is relatively high because the curvature at the start point is zero. The main surprising feature is the presence of three solutions in the middle region. The "middle" branch with $a_1 \approx a_2$ at $c \approx 0$ has the least rms error. Therefore if we wish to minimize error we would follow the bottom branch from $c = 20$ to $c \approx 3.6$, then follow the arrow and jump to the middle branch and follow it to $c \approx -3.6$, then jump again to the top branch and follow it to $c = -20$. This involves discontinuities in both the Bézier arm lengths and the rms error. Figure 4.4 shows the rms error for the ODF calculations, ignoring for the moment the oval path in Fig. 4.3. We have plotted the log of the error to accentuate the minima, and have shown only positive c since the figure is symmetric in c. (Therefore the apparent discontinuities in slope at $c = 0$ will disappear when we unfold the image to include negative c.) It is interesting to note that the overall minimum error does not occur for the circular arc at $c = 0$: it occurs for the slightly asymmetric shape at $c \approx \pm 1.2$. This is somewhat surprising since one might have expected that fitting a symmetric shape would be easier than an asymmetric shape. We will return to this point later when discussing Beta-splines. The main conclusion so far is that the S-shaped solution by itself is unacceptable because of discontinuities. We may need to accept cases where the arm lengths are discontinuous as we vary c, but we should never have to deal with discontinuities in the rms error. To address this issue we now discuss the oval-shaped solution.

The oval-shaped solution can be emulated quite well (see [4] or Sect. 5.1), by calculating the $\langle y' \rangle$-moment of the Bézier curve and searching for extrema of this moment subject to the constraint that the Bézier area must be correct, where the y' axis is defined to be tilted by 22.5° counter-clockwise in Fig. 4.2. Alternatively, it can be stumbled upon "serendipitously" while attempting to solve the ODF equations with a suitably poor initial estimate of **a**. Consider the following sequence of runs. We focus on the area around $c = 3.6$, $a_1 = 57$, where two solutions of the S-shaped branch coalesce and disappear. (This is labelled 'C' in Fig. 4.3). Run the ODF calculation at $c = 3.5$, with an initial estimate **a** = (55.6, 34.3). As expected this converges to the result $\mathbf{a} = (55.5960, 34.3352)$ in 5 iterations, which is on the S-shaped branch. Now perform a run at $c = 4$, with the same initial estimate $\mathbf{a} = (55.6, 34.3)$. We expect this to fail because the solutions have already coalesced; instead, it converges to $\mathbf{a} = (56.2893, 31.9725)$ in 8 iterations. This is the first indication of the new branch, since this solution was not expected. Now go to the opposite extreme, at smaller c. Try $c = 3$, with the same initial estimate $\mathbf{a} = (55.6, 34.3)$. We anticipate this will simply duplicate an existing solution since our initial estimate is between the top two branches of the S-shaped solution. As expected, this converges to $\mathbf{a} = (63.9175, 20.2316)$ in 15 iterations, which is on the topmost branch of the S-shaped solution. However, if we move even farther afield with $c = 2.5$ and the same initial estimate of $\mathbf{a} = (55.6, 34.3)$, we do not get a solution on the S-shaped branch. Instead we get $\mathbf{a} = (60.2117, 28.6692)$ which is in-between the topmost two branches of the S-shaped solution. We will see later that this solution represents a saddle point, not a local minimum. Once the existence of this new branch has been detected we will initialize future runs by using $\mathbf{a}$ values from neighboring runs at similar c values, since we have no other easy way of initializing this calculation. This type of initialization will be used frequently in the following sections where we will encounter even larger numbers of solutions.

4.4   Continuity of the rms Error

We can now resolve the problem of discontinuous rms error as a function of c. Figure 4.4 shows that the oval shaped solution has an rms error that sometimes crosses the results obtained from the S-shaped solution. Therefore, instead of making a discontinuous jump in arm length a_1 at point **C** in Fig. 4.3 where $c = 3.6$, we can follow the path **ABCD** in Fig. 4.4 which uses the new segment **BC** contributed by the oval solution. This gives us the desired continuity in the rms error path from **A** to **D**. These two crossovers of solution branches (points **B** and **C**) are fundamentally different, however: at point **C** the oval solution touches the S-shaped branch tangentially in Fig. 4.4 and the two solutions are identical at this point, while at point **B** in Fig. 4.3, at $c = 6.5$, the solution $\mathbf{a}$ changes discontinuously from $\mathbf{B}_1$ to $\mathbf{B}_2$ as we switch branches.

4.5   Character of Coalescing Solutions

Figure 4.3 shows two instances, points **C** (at $c = 3.6$) and **E** (at $c = 8.5$), where solutions coalesce and disappear. This is always associated with numerical convergence problems due to the fact that the determinant of $\mathbf{M}$ in (2.9) goes through a zero in these cases. Graphically this shows up as a vertical slope in Fig. 4.3, meaning a_i is indeterminate. In practice we deal with this by using increasingly smaller increments in c as we approach the singularity using the previous solution

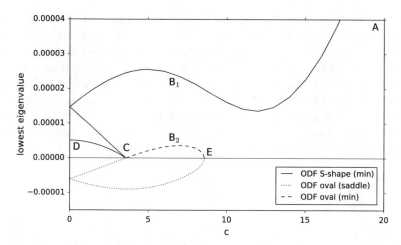

Fig. 4.5 Cubic Bézier lowest eigenvalue

at an old c to initialize the current one. Since the dimension of **M** is small, the calculation of the matrix inverse is relatively free of numerical roundoff error, so this does not pose a serious practical problem. A more instructive view of these merges is provided by the eigenvalues of **M**. Figure 4.5 shows the lowest eigenvalue for each branch as a function of c. Note that this function is symmetric in c, so we will have continuity of the slope at $c = 0$ if we reflect the image to negative c. The S-shaped solution has an eigenvalue that is always the largest (or the three largest) at each value of c, and is always positive, so this solution is consistently a local minimum. The oval shaped solution has an eigenvalue that is locally positive between points **C** (at $c = 3.6$) and **E** (at $c = 8.5$), but is otherwise negative corresponding to a saddle point solution. Note that these saddle point solutions always have the largest rms error whenever we see multiple branches present at the same time in Fig. 4.4. The typical result will be to see a saddle point solution bracketed by two local minima in Fig. 4.3 and having a larger rms error than the two branches associated with it in Fig. 4.4. This behavior will also persist in all the examples to follow, no matter how complex.

   The eigenvalues allow us to make very simple determinations about the nature of the solution. They also assist in distinguishing between types of merges that can occur. For example the merge at point E is a straightforward merge where a saddle point and a local minimum merge and disappear, as can be seen most easily by the simple zero in Fig. 4.5 at $c = 8.5$. On the other hand, the merge at point **C** (at $c = 3.6$) is more complex because it involves three branches, a saddle point and two local minima, coalescing to produce a single local minimum. In either case, though, the rule still is that solutions will always disappear in pairs. With respect to the merge at point **C** it is worth noting that the largest eigenvalue in this pair (not shown) also exhibits the same behavior, meaning that all three values of the largest eigenvalue coalesce at $c = 3.6$, which reinforces the assertion that the solutions are actually identical at this point. This situation is quite rare: only the quartic Bézier in Chap. 8 will show similar behavior. Instead we will typically see many examples of simple merges involving only two solutions, plus numerous examples of avoided crossings where two solutions appear to be merging but then avoid each other at the last minute, presumably due to some coupling between the different branches. It would be interesting to see if it were possible to develop analytical tests to allow us to distinguish a priori between true crossings and avoided crossings, and between simple merges and more complex merges involving three branches. Some preliminary work in this direction is outlined in Chap. 5.

References

1. R.H. Bartels, J.C. Beatty, B.A. Barsky, *An Introduction to Splines for Use in Computer Graphics & Geometric Modeling* (Morgan Kaufmann, Los Altos, 1987)
2. J.D. Foley, A. van Dam, S.K. Feiner, J.F. Hughes, R.L. Phillips, *Introduction to Computer Graphics* (Addison-Wesley, Reading, 1993)
3. J.D. Lawrence, *A Catalog of Special Plane Curves* (Dover, New York, 1972)
4. A. Penner, Fitting a cubic Bezier to a parametric function. Coll. Math. J. **50**, 12 (May 2019, to be published)

Chapter 5
Topology of Merges/Crossovers

This chapter will focus on a series of qualitative arguments that can be used to improve our understanding of the nature of the solutions when they coalesce and disappear, or when they cross each other without any apparent interaction. These qualitative pictures will lead us to a quantitative measure, in the form of a determinant of an augmented matrix, that can be used to diagnose each merge/crossover. The quantitative measure is helpful in diagnosing situations that are more complex than the cubic Bézier fit.

5.1 Center of Mass Fit

In Sect. 4.3 we concluded that the S-shaped solution for the cubic Bézier fit was inadequate due to discontinuities in the rms error. We now note another sense in which it is inadequate, namely describing the topology of solutions when they merge. The S-shaped solution consists exclusively of branches that have been classified as local minima based on their eigenvalues. But we know intuitively that when two local minima coalesce in two dimensions there must be a local maximum between them, if we view the path connecting them in one dimension; or a saddle point, if we view the region between them in two dimensions. Therefore we are missing a critical feature that is needed to describe the topology of the solutions. That feature can be provided by developing a macroscopic criterion that needs to be satisfied in order to provide a good fit. The S-shaped solution in Chap. 4 was initially arrived at by fitting local properties such as curvature. The problem with such an interpretation is that it is an all-or-nothing approach: there is no provision for intermediate results where we are almost, but not quite, successful. A macroscopic fit criterion would be better, since it would allow for the possibility of fits that are not optimal but still topologically interesting by virtue of being worst case scenarios instead of best case. Such a criterion is given by the property of center of mass

© The Author(s), under exclusive license to Springer Nature Switzerland AG 2019
A. Penner, *Fitting Splines to a Parametric Function*,
SpringerBriefs in Computer Science, https://doi.org/10.1007/978-3-030-12551-6_5

(cofm), where the fit can be perfect in some cases but can also smoothly vary to being non-optimal in other cases. Since the center of mass has two independent degrees of freedom, it is well-suited to the study of the cubic Bézier fit of Chap. 4.

For the cofm calculations we follow the development of [4]. Introduce the notation $\langle f \rangle$ to denote the f-moment of an object, where $\langle f \rangle \triangleq \int\int f \, dx \, dy$. We begin by evaluating the area of the closed shape formed by traveling along the Bézier curve from the start to the end, and then returning along a straight line. We use Green's theorem to express this area as a line integral [1, p. 244]: $\langle 1 \rangle = \int\int dx \, dy = \oint x \, dy$. From Eqs. (3.1) and (3.2) we see that the integral will involve all possible linear combinations of the products $x_i y_j$, which are the coordinates of the Bézier control points. The typical integral will be of the type $\int u^i (1 - u)^j \, du$ which can be evaluated using the identity:

$$\int_0^1 u^i (1 - u)^j \, du = i! j! / (i + j + 1)!$$

This identity can be derived either by induction or by integration-by-parts. The final area result is expressible in matrix form: $\langle 1 \rangle = \mathbf{x}^t \mathbf{A} \mathbf{y}$ where $\mathbf{x}^t = (x_0, x_1, x_2, x_3)$, $\mathbf{y}^t = (y_0, y_1, y_2, y_3)$ and

$$\mathbf{A} = 3/20 \begin{pmatrix} 0 & 2 & 1 & -3 \\ -2 & 0 & 1 & 1 \\ -1 & -1 & 0 & 2 \\ 3 & -1 & -2 & 0 \end{pmatrix}.$$

In the notation of Fig. 4.1 and Eqs. (4.1) this can be written as:

$$\langle 1 \rangle = 3/20 \left(2a_1 (l_1 - l_2 \cos \Delta\theta) + 2a_2 (l_2 - l_1 \cos \Delta\theta) - a_1 a_2 \sin \Delta\theta \right) \tag{5.1}$$

where $\Delta\theta = \theta_2 - \theta_1$. We need at least one more constraint in order to evaluate both a_1 and a_2. We get this constraint by evaluating the $\langle y \rangle$ moment. After a great deal of messy, but trivial, algebra, we find the Bézier $\langle y \rangle$ moment is given by the matrix product $\langle y \rangle = \mathbf{y}^t (\mathbf{x}^t \mathbf{D} \mathbf{y}) / 280$ where $\mathbf{x}$ and $\mathbf{y}$ are the Bézier coordinate vectors and $\mathbf{D}$ is the vertical array of matrices:

$$\begin{pmatrix} 0 & 35 & 10 & -45 \\ -35 & 0 & 12 & 23 \\ -10 & -12 & 0 & 22 \\ 45 & -23 & -22 & 0 \end{pmatrix}, \quad \begin{pmatrix} 0 & 15 & 3 & -18 \\ -15 & 0 & 9 & 6 \\ -3 & -9 & 0 & 12 \\ 18 & -6 & -12 & 0 \end{pmatrix},$$

$$\begin{pmatrix} 0 & 12 & 6 & -18 \\ -12 & 0 & 9 & 3 \\ -6 & -9 & 0 & 15 \\ 18 & -3 & -15 & 0 \end{pmatrix}, \quad \begin{pmatrix} 0 & 22 & 23 & -45 \\ -22 & 0 & 12 & 10 \\ -23 & -12 & 0 & 35 \\ 45 & -10 & -35 & 0 \end{pmatrix}.$$

With these expressions we could, as in [4], fit the center of mass by calculating $\langle x \rangle / \langle 1 \rangle$ and $\langle y \rangle / \langle 1 \rangle$ for the Bézier curve, $\mathbf{f}(u)$, and equating them to the corresponding properties of the hypoTrochoid function, $\mathbf{g}(t)$. However, a simpler method can be developed by using the symmetry properties of the hypoTrochoid. First, rotate the coordinate system in Fig. 4.2 counter-clockwise by 22.5°, and denote the new y-axis by y'. Now we have an object that inverts itself in the (tilted) y' axis when we change the sign of c. Therefore the $\langle y' \rangle$ moment of the tilted object is anti-symmetric in c, while the area, $\langle 1 \rangle$, is symmetric. We will fit these two properties of the object since they are qualitatively different, and are easy to calculate. In the notation of (4.1) we can write $\langle y' \rangle$ as:

$$
\begin{aligned}
280 \langle y' \rangle = {} & a_1(l_1 - l_2 \cos \Delta\theta)(-50l_1 + 34l_2) \sin(\Delta\theta/2) \\
& + a_2(l_2 - l_1 \cos \Delta\theta)(-34l_1 + 50l_2) \sin(\Delta\theta/2) \\
& + a_1 a_2(l_1 - l_2)(21 \sin \Delta\theta \sin(\Delta\theta/2) - 12(1 + \cos \Delta\theta) \cos(\Delta\theta/2)) \\
& + 15a_1^2(l_1 - l_2 \cos \Delta\theta) \cos(\Delta\theta/2) - 15a_2^2(l_2 - l_1 \cos \Delta\theta) \cos(\Delta\theta/2) \\
& + 9a_1 a_2^2 \sin \Delta\theta \cos(\Delta\theta/2) - 9a_1^2 a_2 \sin \Delta\theta \cos(\Delta\theta/2)
\end{aligned}
$$

$$(5.2)$$

We note in passing that the expression for area is symmetric with respect to simultaneous interchange of the variables (a_1, l_1) with (a_2, l_2), while the $\langle y' \rangle$ moment is anti-symmetric with respect to this operation. These properties are consistent with the anti-symmetry of the (tilted) hypoTrochoid with respect to c. To implement these equations, we evaluate $\langle 1 \rangle$ and $\langle y' \rangle$ for the hypoTrochoid, $\mathbf{g}(t)$, and substitute these values into the left hand side of (5.1) and (5.2). Since (5.1) is linear in a_2, we solve it for a_2 and substitute this into (5.2) to obtain a quartic equation for a_1. Solving this, we obtain an S-shaped solution which is qualitatively the same as the result obtained from the curvature fit in Fig. 4.3, as well as the S-shaped solution in [4, Fig. 6], which was obtained by fitting the center of mass. So far we have not yet produced any new information concerning the nature of the solutions when they coalesce. Now we make the following observation: consider the one-dimensional problem obtained when we constrain the area to be correct at all times while we vary a_1 or a_2. Then it is reasonable to assume that the solutions that perfectly fit $\langle y' \rangle$ would correspond at least approximately to local minima of the rms error along this one-dimensional path, while the region between any two such solutions would necessarily correspond to a local maximum, or a saddle point in two dimensions. Therefore, if we have two solutions of the $\langle y' \rangle$ equation that are close to each other, and if we search between them for an extremum of the function $\langle y' \rangle$, subject to the constraint that the area must be correct, we expect that this extremum will roughly correspond to a saddle point between them. On the other hand, if the two solutions have already coalesced and disappeared, then the extremum of $\langle y' \rangle$ should correspond to a distance of closest approach to the point where the solutions disappeared, in which case it should represent a local minimum. To find these extrema we differentiate (5.2) with respect to a_2, and set the result to zero. This removes the left hand side since it is constant, and lowers the order of the equation by one. The new equation contains the unknown da_1/da_2, which we calculate by differentiating the constraint in (5.1), and substituting it into our equation. This brings the order of the equation back to where it was before, and when we solve this equation simultaneously with (5.1) we obtain a new quartic equation which the extrema of $\langle y' \rangle$ will satisfy. The solutions are given in [4, Fig. 6], showing both the extremized $\langle y' \rangle$ results at a fixed area (entitled "max<y>@<1>"), and the ODF results. The extrema of $\langle y' \rangle$ yield an oval-shaped solution which agrees very well with the corresponding solution obtained from the ODF method. This method could therefore serve as a good initial estimate for the ODF calculation, and was often used as such in Chap. 4. However, it is the topological properties that we are specifically interested in here. This method suggests a mechanism by which three branches (two minima plus a saddle point) could coalesce, but it implies that all three branches must necessarily merge at the same time. If the constrained function $\langle y' \rangle$ is approximately a parabola, and if we slowly lift it or lower it to make two roots coalesce then it is clear that the saddle point will lie in the exact center of the two roots and that all three points will merge at one point. This may be an unnecessarily restrictive view of the situation.

An alternative view of the same problem is obtained if we imagine moving along the one-dimensional path that leads from one local minimum to another in the two-dimensional contour map of the rms error. As we do so, we can model the rms error as being a quartic polynomial, which is the simplest model that has two minima and one local maximum. However, if we wish both minima and the local maximum to coalesce at the same point, it is necessary to assume arbitrarily that the two local minima have exactly the same height. This is unnecessarily restrictive, since we have no physical basis for making such an assumption. We therefore suspect that the correct picture may be more complicated than this.

5.2   Example of Two Types of Merge/Crossover

Figure 5.1 shows the ODF results for the cubic Bézier at the point C in Fig. 4.3, where three solutions are apparently merging at a single point. We have zoomed in considerably to focus on the range $3.58 < c < 3.605$. The arm length a_1 shows that this is not a simultaneous merge of three solutions, but is instead two separate events, both of which involve only two branches at a time. The first event, which we will term a *Type 1 merge*, has an eigenvalue of zero, Fig. 5.1b, after which the solutions disappear. This type of event also occurs at $c = 8.5$ for the cubic Bézier fit, and will re-occur many times in the examples to follow. The second event, which we will call a *Type 2 crossover*, also has a zero eigenvalue, but the solutions do not disappear: instead they interchange character so that a minimum becomes a saddle point and vice-versa. This type of event is very rare, and we have found only one other instance of its' occurrence: in the quartic Bézier fit (Chap. 8). The close proximity of these two events explains why the S-shaped solution appears as

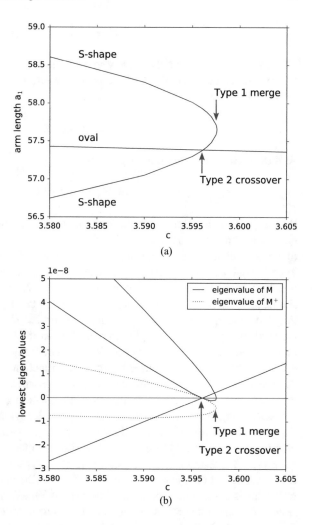

Fig. 5.1 Cubic Bézier solution crossings. (**a**) Arm length. (**b**) Eigenvalues

a minimum over virtually all its lifetime, by going through two changes of form in very quick succession at $c = 3.596$ and $c = 3.5975$. It is gratifying to see that these changes are occurring smoothly, since otherwise we would have had to postulate a cusp in the S-shaped solution at this point, which would be difficult to model.

We wish to qualitatively model these two types of events, to see if we can distinguish between them. This can be done using the concepts of catastrophe theory. In this theory, the merge of a minimum and a saddle point is classified as a *fold catastrophe* [3, 5]. Assume that the rms error has the form of a cubic curve as we move along the one-dimensional path that joins the critical points of the error functional $F(\mathbf{a}, u)$. This is the simplest curve that can simulate the merge of a minimum with a saddle point. The cubic curve is given by

$$F = x^3 + qx$$

where we are interested only in the shape of the curve, and have therefore removed all parameters that affect only the scaling and positioning. If this curve has two real extrema, then they will be located at x_e, where

$$x_e = \pm\sqrt{-q/3}.$$

At these extrema the curvature is given by

$$k_e = 6x_e = \pm\sqrt{-12q}. \tag{5.3}$$

Recall the fact that the eigenvalues of the $\mathbf{M}$ matrix (Sect. 2.2) are equal to the curvature of the $F(\mathbf{a}, u)$ functional at the critical points. Therefore (5.3) allows us to make qualitative predictions about the behavior of the eigenvalues of $\mathbf{M}$. For a Type 1 event we assume that the parameter q is a linear function of the c parameter which controls the shape of $\mathbf{g}(t)$: assume $q = c - c_0$. In this case the eigenvalues should have the following three properties: for $c > c_0$ they cease to exist, for $c < c_0$ they have the appearance of a parabola tilted on its' side by $90°$, and in all cases they will be symmetrically split from zero when they are non-degenerate. All of these properties are exhibited by the Type 1 event in Fig. 5.1. On the other hand, for a Type 2 event, we assume that q is a quadratic function of c: $q = -(c - c_0)^2$. Then we have the following predictions: the eigenvalues will be linear functions of c, they will cross each other at $c = c_0$ (with a possible relabeling required since a minimum is transforming into a saddle point), and they will be symmetrically split from zero. These properties are all exhibited by the Type 2 crossing in Fig. 5.1. The Type 2 crossing also has one additional feature, which is that satisfying the requirements for a Type 2 crossing is more difficult than for a Type 1 merge. A Type 2 crossing requires that, not only is $q = 0$ at $c = c_0$, but also the first derivative, q', is zero as well. This is consistent with the finding that the Type 2 crossing is very rare in our results. It means that an extra requirement must be satisfied, in addition to the Type 1 requirements. In the next section, we will quantify that requirement.

5.3   Response to Change in g(t)

The previous section provided a qualitative picture of how two crossings might differ. It is difficult to convert this into a quantitative model because it would require taking third derivatives of F. Here we use a different approach, which is to predict quantitatively the response of the solution to a change in c, which controls the shape of $\mathbf{g}(t)$. It is clear that this response will be different in the two cases because the slope in Fig. 5.1a is infinite for a Type 1 merge.

Starting from (2.7), we wish to evaluate the response $dL_i/dc \triangleq d^2F/da_i dc$ subject to the constraints that $L_i = 0$ and (2.1) are both satisfied at all times. First re-express L_i:

$$L_i = \int_{t_1}^{t_2} \mathcal{I}_i(c, \mathbf{a}, u)dt$$

where $\mathcal{I}_i(c, \mathbf{a}, u) \triangleq (f_x(u) - g_x(t))\partial f_x/\partial a_i + (f_y(u) - g_y(t))\partial f_y/\partial a_i$.

$$\therefore dL_i/dc = \int_{t_1}^{t_2} \left[\partial \mathcal{I}_i/\partial c + \sum_{j=1}^{n} \partial \mathcal{I}_i/\partial a_j(\partial a_j/\partial c) + \partial \mathcal{I}_i/\partial u(du/dc) \right] dt$$

(5.4)

Now note that du/dc can be re-expressed as:

$$du/dc = \partial u/\partial c + \sum_{j=1}^{n} \partial u/\partial a_j(\partial a_j/\partial c)$$

$$\therefore dL_i/dc = \int_{t_1}^{t_2} \left[\partial \mathcal{I}_i/\partial c + \sum_{j=1}^{n}(\partial \mathcal{I}_i/\partial a_j + \partial \mathcal{I}_i/\partial u(\partial u/\partial a_j))(\partial a_j/\partial c) \right.$$
$$\left. + \partial \mathcal{I}_i/\partial u(\partial u/\partial c) \right] dt$$

Imposing the constraint $dL_i/dc = 0$ and recognizing that the term in the summation is just the definition of G_{ij}, we can write this as a matrix equation:

$$\mathbf{M}(d\mathbf{a}/dc) + \mathbf{Y} = 0 \tag{5.5}$$

where $d\mathbf{a}/dc = \{\partial a_i/\partial c\}$ and the column vector $\mathbf{Y}$ is given by:

$$Y_i = \int_{t_1}^{t_2} \left[\partial \mathcal{I}_i/\partial c + \partial \mathcal{I}_i/\partial u(\partial u/\partial c) \right] dt.$$

This allows us to calculate the response functions $d\mathbf{a}/dc$, which are the slopes in Fig. 5.1a. We must, however, first calculate $\partial u/\partial c$, which follows the same method used to get (2.3). The result is:

$$E(u)\partial u/\partial c = - f_x'(u)\partial(f_x(u) - g_x(t))/\partial c - (f_x(u) - g_x(t))\partial f_x'(u)/\partial c$$
$$- f_y'(u)\partial(f_y(u) - g_y(t))/\partial c - (f_y(u) - g_y(t))\partial f_y'(u)/\partial c.$$

Now recall the definition of $\mathcal{I}_i$ in (5.4) and write out the integrand of Y_i explicitly to get $Y_i = \int_{t_1}^{t_2} [d\mathcal{I}_i/dc]dt$ where

$$dI_i/dc \triangleq \partial I_i/\partial c + \partial I_i/\partial u(\partial u/\partial c)$$

$$= \left[\partial(f_x(u) - g_x(t))/\partial c + f_x'(u)(\partial u/\partial c)\right]\partial f_x/\partial a_i$$

$$+ (f_x(u) - g_x(t))\left[\partial^2 f_x/\partial c\partial a_i + \partial f_x'/\partial a_i(\partial u/\partial c)\right]$$

$$+ \left[\partial(f_y(u) - g_y(t))/\partial c + f_y'(u)(\partial u/\partial c)\right]\partial f_y/\partial a_i$$

$$+ (f_y(u) - g_y(t))\left[\partial^2 f_y/\partial c\partial a_i + \partial f_y'/\partial a_i(\partial u/\partial c)\right]$$

Note that the derivative dI_i/dc has been evaluated at a variable $u(t)$ but fixed **a**. Now we can substitute (2.3) into this equation to obtain the simplified result:

$$dI_i/dc = \partial f_x/\partial a_i\left[\partial(f_x(u) - g_x(t))/\partial c\right] + (f_x(u) - g_x(t))\left[\partial^2 f_x/\partial c\partial a_i\right]$$

$$+ \partial f_y/\partial a_i\left[\partial(f_y(u) - g_y(t))/\partial c\right] + (f_y(u) - g_y(t))\left[\partial^2 f_y/\partial c\partial a_i\right]$$

$$- E(u)\partial u/\partial a_i(\partial u/\partial c)$$

This has essentially the same form as (2.8). As before, the Hessian terms $\partial^2 f_x/\partial c\partial a_i$ and $\partial^2 f_y/\partial c\partial a_i$ will be zero for most splines, except for the Beta-splines. We can now perform the necessary numerical integrations and implement (5.5). Numerical comparisons of (5.5) with finite difference estimates of $d\mathbf{a}/dc$ have shown that it correctly calculates this response, even close to Type 1 merges, so it could potentially be very useful in extrapolating from one solution to the next as we vary c. However, we wish to make a slightly different use of it, as a diagnostic tool in the next section.

5.4   Distinguishing Between Type 1 and Type 2 Events

The Type 1 and Type 2 events share the fact that the determinant of **M** is zero in both cases. On the other hand, the Type 1 merge is unique in that it has infinite slope $d\mathbf{a}/dc$. We wish to use this fact to distinguish between them. Consider the case where **M** is singular. In this case there must be a linear combination of its' rows that produces a zero row. Assume that the coefficients in this linear combination are the sequence $\{l_i\}_{i=1}^n \triangleq \mathbf{l}$. If we apply this same linear combination to the elements of the vector **Y** to form $\mathbf{l} \cdot \mathbf{Y}$, then the typical result will be nonzero, in which case the solution (5.5) for that row, da_i/dc, would be infinite due to division by zero. This yields a Type 1 merge. On the other hand, if the result is zero, then $da_i/dc = 0/0$, which may be well-behaved, depending on the details of the calculation. In any event, we will take this zero as an indicator of a Type 2 crossover. To detect this occurrence of zero we form the augmented matrix $\mathbf{M}^+$:

$$\mathbf{M}_{ij}^{+} = \mathbf{M}_{ij} \text{ for } \{i, j\} \in \{1, n\}$$

$$\mathbf{M}_{i,n+1}^{+} = \mathbf{M}_{n+1,i}^{+} = \mathbf{Y}_i \text{ for } i \in \{1, n\}$$

$$\mathbf{M}_{n+1,n+1}^{+} = d^2 F/dc^2$$

The term $d^2 F/dc^2$ can be expressed as $d^2 F/dc^2 \triangleq \int_{t_1}^{t_2} \mathcal{J} dt$, and is derived the same way as (2.8) and Y_i, to obtain

$$\mathcal{J} = \left[\partial(f_x(u) - g_x(t))/\partial c \right]^2 + (f_x(u) - g_x(t)) \left[\partial^2 f_x/\partial c^2 \right]$$
$$+ \left[\partial(f_y(u) - g_y(t))/\partial c \right]^2 + (f_y(u) - g_y(t)) \left[\partial^2 f_y/\partial c^2 \right]$$
$$- E(u)\partial u/\partial c(\partial u/\partial c).$$

From the construction of $\mathbf{M}^{+}$ we see that, if $\mathbf{M}$ is singular and if the linear combination $\mathbf{l} \cdot \mathbf{Y}$ is also zero, then $\mathbf{M}^{+}$ will be singular. This is a sufficient condition, but not necessary.

In effect, $\mathbf{M}^{+}$ is the second-order response matrix we would get if we introduced c as a new independent variable, treated the same way as the existing variables in $\mathbf{a}$. The only difference is that the ODF solutions are defined such that F is stationary with respect to changes in $\mathbf{a}$, but not with respect to c. The augmented matrix has been defined to be symmetric so that its eigenvalues are real. (It appears to play the same role as a similar matrix defined in [2, p. 66, while deriving Lemma 9]). Based on the previous discussion, we now anticipate that a zero eigenvalue in $\mathbf{M}^{+}$ will correspond to a Type 2 crossover, assuming that $\mathbf{M}$ is also singular. There are three distinct situations that can occur: only $\mathbf{M}$ is singular (Type 1 merge), both $\mathbf{M}$ and $\mathbf{M}^{+}$ are singular (Type 2 crossover), or only $\mathbf{M}^{+}$ is singular, which is of no particular interest.

As an aside, we note that the situation in which $\mathbf{M}$ and $\mathbf{M}^{+}$ are simultaneously singular appears to be in conflict with [2, Assumption A, p. 60]. The argument in [2] is based on consideration of number of degrees of freedom versus constraints. The resolution of this conflict will be attempted elsewhere, since it is somewhat outside the scope of this article, which is primarily computational in nature, not theoretical.

The lowest eigenvalues of $\mathbf{M}^{+}$ are shown in Fig. 5.1b, for all three branches of the solution. We see that they are zero as expected for the Type 2 crossover, along with the eigenvalues of $\mathbf{M}$. The Type 1 merge is characterized by only a single zero, in the eigenvalues of $\mathbf{M}$. It is worth noting that the Type 2 crossover consists of two branches which cross each other: one branch is the S-shaped solution whose eigenvalues have a negative slope at this point. For this branch the eigenvalues of $\mathbf{M}$ and $\mathbf{M}^{+}$ are easily distinguishable since they touch only tangentially. The other branch is the oval-shaped shaped solution whose eigenvalues have a positive slope at this point. For this branch the eigenvalues of $\mathbf{M}$ and $\mathbf{M}^{+}$ are essentially indistinguishable.

We therefore have a complete diagnostic procedure, capable of distinguishing between the different types of topology changes that can occur. A similar test will also be performed on the eigenvalues of the quartic Bézier in Chap. 8, with a similar result. In Chap. 7 the 6-point B-spline yields an interesting example of how the eigenvalues of $\mathbf{M}^+$ behave in the presence of a narrowly avoided crossing.

References

1. T.M. Apostol, *Calculus*, vol. II (Blaisdell, New York, 1961)
2. J.-P. Aubin, I. Ekeland, *Applied Nonlinear Analysis* (Dover, New York, 2006)
3. L. Florack, A. Kuijper, The topological structure of scale-space images. J. Math. Imaging Vis. **12**, 65–79 (2000)
4. A. Penner, Fitting a cubic Bezier to a parametric function. Coll. Math. J. **50**, 12 (May 2019, to be published)
5. T. Poston, I. Stewart, *Catastrophe Theory and Its Applications* (Dover, New York, 1996)

Chapter 6
ODF Using a 5-Point B-Spline

When we chose the family of hypoTrochoid curves as a test of the fitting method, it was felt that there were two features of this family that might be challenging: namely the quartic nature of the curve in the presence of a double inflection point, which cannot be properly modeled by a cubic Bézier, and the change in symmetry from a highly asymmetric shape at $c = \pm 20$ to a symmetric (circular) shape at $c = 0$. Of these two, it appears that the double inflection point has not caused a major problem since the fit at $c = \pm 10$ in Fig. 4.4, for example, is not much different than the fit at $c = \pm 20$. However, the change in symmetry has caused a major problem. It has been necessary to use three types of solution: one asymmetric branch of the S-shaped solution at $c = \pm 20$, plus one symmetric branch of the S-shaped solution at $c \approx 0$, plus a bridge between them which comes from a qualitatively new oval-shaped solution. The resulting discontinuous jumps in $\mathbf{a}$ between these branches would lead to many practical problems if we were attempting some kind of animation to produce a smooth transition from one shape to another. Therefore we need to investigate other types of splines to see if we can eliminate these discontinuities.

The simplest extension of the cubic Bézier is to add a new knot and a control point in the middle to get a 5-point B-spline. The new knot vector will be $U = (0\,0\,0\\ 0\,1\,2\,2\,2\,2)$. This represents a cubic spline with two segments and 5 control points. The endpoints $\mathbf{Q}_0$ and $\mathbf{Q}_4$ will be the same as before, and the intermediate control points are given by

$$\mathbf{Q}_1 = (x_1, y_1) = (x_0 - a_1 \sin\theta_1,\ y_0 + a_1 \cos\theta_1)$$

$$\mathbf{Q}_2 = (x_2, y_2)$$

$$\mathbf{Q}_3 = (x_3, y_3) = (x_4 + a_2 \sin\theta_2,\ y_4 - a_2 \cos\theta_2).$$

The parameter vector has four degrees of freedom: $\mathbf{a} \triangleq (a_1, a_2, x_2, y_2)$. It is hoped that the presence of the new adjustable point $\mathbf{Q}_2$ might give us the ability to smoothly transition from an asymmetric to a symmetric shape.

© The Author(s), under exclusive license to Springer Nature Switzerland AG 2019
A. Penner, *Fitting Splines to a Parametric Function*,
SpringerBriefs in Computer Science, https://doi.org/10.1007/978-3-030-12551-6_6

6.1   Initializing a 5-Point B-Spline

We wish to use a previously calculated cubic Bézier to initialize an equivalent B-spline representation. Assume that the cubic Bézier had the knot vector $U = (0\,0\,0\,0\,2\,2\,2\,2)$; then the relationship between the B-spline control points $\mathbf{Q}$ and the Bézier control points $\mathbf{P}$ is (3.4):

$$\begin{pmatrix} \mathbf{Q}_0 \\ \mathbf{Q}_1 \\ \mathbf{Q}_2 \\ \mathbf{Q}_3 \\ \mathbf{Q}_4 \end{pmatrix} = \begin{pmatrix} 1 & 0 & 0 & 0 \\ \frac{1}{2} & \frac{1}{2} & 0 & 0 \\ 0 & \frac{1}{2} & \frac{1}{2} & 0 \\ 0 & 0 & \frac{1}{2} & \frac{1}{2} \\ 0 & 0 & 0 & 1 \end{pmatrix} \begin{pmatrix} \mathbf{P}_0 \\ \mathbf{P}_1 \\ \mathbf{P}_2 \\ \mathbf{P}_3 \end{pmatrix} \tag{6.1}$$

This can be interpreted simply to mean that the B-spline arm lengths a_1 and a_2 will (initially) be half the Bézier arm lengths, and that the new B-spline control point $\mathbf{Q}_2$ will be the average of the existing Bézier points $\mathbf{P}_1$ and $\mathbf{P}_2$. The change in arm lengths, in turn, can be attributed to the fact that there are now two segments instead of one, so the relative arm length, compared to the knot interval, has not actually changed. This allows us to use the numerical results from Chap. 4 to start the ODF calculation.

6.2   Basis Functions of a 5-Point B-Spline

The basis functions for the 5-point B-spline are obtained from (3.3):

	for $0 < u < 1$	for $1 < u < 2$
$N_{03} =$	$(1-u)^3$	0
$N_{13} =$	$u(12 - 18u + 7u^2)/4$	$(2-u)^3/4$
$N_{23} =$	$u^2(3 - 2u)/2$	$(2-u)^2(2u-1)/2$
$N_{33} =$	$u^3/4$	$(2-u)(7u^2 - 10u + 4)/4$
$N_{43} =$	0	$(u-1)^3$

The functions $N_{i3}(u)$ are defined as two separate segments, but we note that $N_{i3}(u)$, $N'_{i3}(u)$, and $N''_{i3}(u)$ are all continuous at $u = 1$, as is required for C^2 continuity. This particular form is suitable for numerical computation but is otherwise not very informative. A much more interesting representation is obtained if we re-express these as linear combinations of Bernstein polynomials, in which case we get:

$$\begin{pmatrix} N_{03} \\ N_{13} \\ N_{23} \\ N_{33} \end{pmatrix} = \begin{pmatrix} 1 & 0 & 0 & 0 \\ 0 & 1 & \frac{1}{2} & \frac{1}{4} \\ 0 & 0 & \frac{1}{2} & \frac{1}{2} \\ 0 & 0 & 0 & \frac{1}{4} \end{pmatrix} \begin{pmatrix} B_{03}(u) \\ B_{13}(u) \\ B_{23}(u) \\ B_{33}(u) \end{pmatrix} \quad \text{for } 0 < u < 1 \qquad (6.2)$$

and

$$\begin{pmatrix} N_{13} \\ N_{23} \\ N_{33} \\ N_{43} \end{pmatrix} = \begin{pmatrix} \frac{1}{4} & 0 & 0 & 0 \\ \frac{1}{2} & \frac{1}{2} & 0 & 0 \\ \frac{1}{4} & \frac{1}{2} & 1 & 0 \\ 0 & 0 & 0 & 1 \end{pmatrix} \begin{pmatrix} B_{03}(u-1) \\ B_{13}(u-1) \\ B_{23}(u-1) \\ B_{33}(u-1) \end{pmatrix} \quad \text{for } 1 < u < 2. \qquad (6.3)$$

We will refer back to this representation later, since it is closely related to the transform obtained for control points (6.4).

6.3 Decomposition into Two Bézier Segments

With the basis functions known, the ODF calculation proceeds the same as in Chap. 4, except for the increase in the number of unknowns. Once the optimization is complete, we may wish to express the results in the form of two Bézier segments, for the purpose of easily rendering the result using a vector-graphics program such as Inkscape. To do so, use (3.4) recursively to convert the knot vector $U = (0\ 0\ 0\ 0\ 1\ 2\ 2\ 2\ 2)$ into the vector $U = (0\ 0\ 0\ 0\ 1\ 1\ 1\ 1\ 2\ 2\ 2\ 2)$ which represents two disjoint Bézier segments. The relationship between the original five B-spline control points $\mathbf{Q}$ and the eight new Bézier control points $\mathbf{R}$ is given by:

$$\begin{pmatrix} \mathbf{R}_0 \\ \mathbf{R}_1 \\ \mathbf{R}_2 \\ \mathbf{R}_3 \\ \mathbf{R}_4 \\ \mathbf{R}_5 \\ \mathbf{R}_6 \\ \mathbf{R}_7 \end{pmatrix} = \begin{pmatrix} 1 & 0 & 0 & 0 & 0 \\ 0 & 1 & 0 & 0 & 0 \\ 0 & \frac{1}{2} & \frac{1}{2} & 0 & 0 \\ 0 & \frac{1}{4} & \frac{1}{2} & \frac{1}{4} & 0 \\ 0 & \frac{1}{4} & \frac{1}{2} & \frac{1}{4} & 0 \\ 0 & 0 & \frac{1}{2} & \frac{1}{2} & 0 \\ 0 & 0 & 0 & 1 & 0 \\ 0 & 0 & 0 & 0 & 1 \end{pmatrix} \begin{pmatrix} \mathbf{Q}_0 \\ \mathbf{Q}_1 \\ \mathbf{Q}_2 \\ \mathbf{Q}_3 \\ \mathbf{Q}_4 \end{pmatrix} \qquad (6.4)$$

We will use this whenever we decide to render the curve, although otherwise it is not really needed. The disjoint nature of the representation can be seen by the fact that the end point $\mathbf{R}_3$ of the first segment is identical to the start point $\mathbf{R}_4$ of the second segment. Since these are independent variables, we can now physically separate the two segments if desired.

Apart from its' practical significance in rendering the curve, (6.4) also has some theoretical significance. We note that the matrix is block diagonal with the diagonal blocks consisting of two 4×4 matrices. The 4×4 matrix at the upper left is the transpose of the transform in (6.2), and the 4×4 matrix at the bottom right is the transpose of the transform in (6.3). We therefore have a link between the transform properties of the control points and the transform properties of the basis functions. This is interesting because calculating the transform properties of control points (3.4) is considerably easier than the same task in the basis functions (3.3).

Here we will try to formalize this relationship. This is not intended as a mathematical proof, but rather an after-the-fact rationalization of a relationship that has already been established. Note that, since (6.4) is block diagonal, it can be written as two separate relationships of the type:

$$\mathbf{R} = \mathbf{AQ}$$

where $\mathbf{R}$ (and $\mathbf{Q}$) are column vectors representing four Bézier (and four B-spline) control points, and $\mathbf{A}$ is a 4×4 constant matrix. If we were to evaluate the spline (using the Bézier representation) at this point we would use the notation

$$\mathbf{f}(u) = \mathbf{B}^t(u)\mathbf{R}$$

where $\mathbf{B}(u)$ is a column vector with Bernstein polynomials $B_{ip}(u)$. This can now be rewritten as

$$\mathbf{f}(u) = \mathbf{B}^t(u)\mathbf{R} = \mathbf{B}^t(u)\mathbf{AQ} = (\mathbf{A}^t\mathbf{B}(u))^t\mathbf{Q}.$$

Now, if we expressed this same function $\mathbf{f}(u)$ in terms of B-spline basis functions we would use the notation

$$\mathbf{f}(u) = \mathbf{N}^t(u)\mathbf{Q}$$

where $\mathbf{N}(u)$ is a column vector with elements $N_{ip}(u)$, which are B-spline basis functions. Equating these two expressions we get

$$\mathbf{N}(u) = \mathbf{A}^t\mathbf{B}(u) \tag{6.5}$$

which is exactly the relationship observed above, when comparing the two versions of $\mathbf{A}$ to (6.2), (6.3). Note that this is true separately for both segments, and that it will also turn out to be true for the three segment, six-point, B-spline in Chap. 7. If nothing else, this relationship serves as a non-trivial test of internal consistency in the calculations, since the calculation of basis functions can be rather lengthy.

6.4   ODF Results for a 5-Point B-Spline

Figure 6.1 shows the arm length a_1 for this B-spline; where, as before, $a_2(c) = a_1(-c)$. The new variables x_2 and y_2 are not shown since they do not contain any qualitatively new information. Figure 6.1 is significantly simpler than Fig. 4.3, in that there is only one main branch of interest. There is a disconnected oval-shaped solution close to the origin, which may be a remnant of the oval-shaped solution from the Bézier fit, but it is of no interest since it does not lead to a low rms error. The rms error is shown in Fig. 6.2. At $c = 20$ the 5-point B-spline fit is better than the cubic Bézier fit by a factor of about 5, and at $c = 0$ it is better by a factor of about 6. Both fits share a common feature, which is a global minimum at $c \approx 1.2$, not at $c = 0$. At a first glance it appears that we have been successful in producing a fit that is continuously variable over the whole range of c. However, on closer inspection,

Fig. 6.1 5-point B-spline arm length a_1

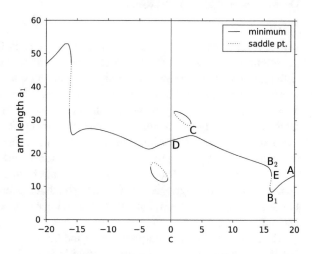

Fig. 6.2 5-point B-spline rms error

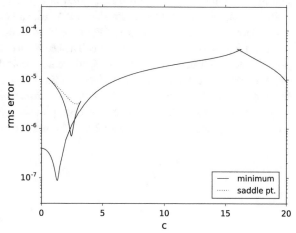

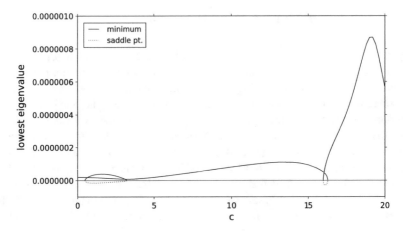

Fig. 6.3 5-point B-spline lowest eigenvalue

we see a glitch at $c \approx 16$. There is a small range of c, from 16.0 to 16.2, where the solution temporarily becomes a saddle point, and we have an S-shaped response with three possible solutions. The nature of the glitch is not nearly as serious as it was in the cubic Bézier fit: we do not have to invoke an entirely new type of solution in order to bridge the gap between solutions. Instead, in Fig. 6.2 it is possible to maintain continuity of the rms error just by moving from the bottom portion of the S-shape to the top portion, which was not possible in Fig. 4.4. However, the discontinuous jump required in the value of a_1 is still quite significant, so we cannot say that the problem of discontinuous response has been solved. We see that overall there is a rather good agreement between the qualitative features of Figs. 4.3 and 6.1. For example the points $\mathbf{AB_1B_2CDE}$ in Fig. 4.3 correspond well to the same points marked in Fig. 6.1.

The above qualitative interpretation of the behavior around the discontinuity is confirmed by the lowest eigenvalue, plotted in Fig. 6.3. This shows a small saddle point region, with a negative eigenvalue at $c \approx 16$, and another one in the range $1 < c < 3$. However, the apparent crossing of the lowest eigenvalues of two branches at $c = 1$ and 3 is not in any way significant. The second lowest eigenvalues (not shown) do not touch each other at these points, so the solutions do not actually cross.

In summary, we conclude that the 5-point B-spline has not entirely solved the problem of how to make a smooth transition from an asymmetric limit to a symmetric shape. This is somewhat disappointing, given that we doubled the number of degrees of freedom, from 2 to 4, in order to perform this fit.

Chapter 7
ODF Using a 6-Point B-Spline

Since the addition of one control point was somewhat successful in smoothing the response to changes in the shape of the hypoTrochoid, we now consider a 6-point B-spline with yet another new knot and control point. The new knot vector will be $U = (0\,0\,0\,0\,1\,2\,3\,3\,3\,3)$. This represents a cubic spline with three segments and 6 control points. The endpoints $\mathbf{Q}_0$ and $\mathbf{Q}_5$ will be the same as before, and the intermediate control points are given by

$$\mathbf{Q}_1 = (x_1, y_1) = (x_0 - a_1 \sin\theta_1, y_0 + a_1 \cos\theta_1)$$

$$\mathbf{Q}_2 = (x_2, y_2)$$

$$\mathbf{Q}_3 = (x_3, y_3)$$

$$\mathbf{Q}_4 = (x_4, y_4) = (x_5 + a_2 \sin\theta_2, y_5 - a_2 \cos\theta_2).$$

The parameter vector has six degrees of freedom: $\mathbf{a} \triangleq (a_1, a_2, x_2, y_2, x_3, y_3)$.

7.1 Initializing a 6-Point B-Spline

As before, we will use a previously calculated cubic Bézier to initialize the B-spline calculation. Assume that the cubic Bézier had the knot vector $U = (0\,0\,0\,0\,3\,3\,3\,3)$; then the relationship between the B-spline control points $\mathbf{Q}$ and the Bézier control points $\mathbf{P}$ is (3.4):

© The Author(s), under exclusive license to Springer Nature Switzerland AG 2019
A. Penner, *Fitting Splines to a Parametric Function*,
SpringerBriefs in Computer Science, https://doi.org/10.1007/978-3-030-12551-6_7

$$\begin{pmatrix} \mathbf{Q}_0 \\ \mathbf{Q}_1 \\ \mathbf{Q}_2 \\ \mathbf{Q}_3 \\ \mathbf{Q}_4 \\ \mathbf{Q}_5 \end{pmatrix} = \begin{pmatrix} 1 & 0 & 0 & 0 \\ \frac{2}{3} & \frac{1}{3} & 0 & 0 \\ \frac{2}{9} & \frac{5}{9} & \frac{2}{9} & 0 \\ 0 & \frac{2}{9} & \frac{5}{9} & \frac{2}{9} \\ 0 & 0 & \frac{1}{3} & \frac{2}{3} \\ 0 & 0 & 0 & 1 \end{pmatrix} \begin{pmatrix} \mathbf{P}_0 \\ \mathbf{P}_1 \\ \mathbf{P}_2 \\ \mathbf{P}_3 \end{pmatrix}$$

This can be interpreted to mean that the (initial) B-spline arm lengths a_1 and a_2 will be one third the Bézier arm lengths, and that the new B-spline control points $\mathbf{Q}_2$ and $\mathbf{Q}_3$ will be somewhat more complicated interpolated values of the points $\mathbf{P}_0$ to $\mathbf{P}_3$. The change in arm lengths can be attributed to the fact that there are now three segments instead of one, so the relative arm length, compared to the knot interval, has not actually changed. As before, we will use the numerical results from Chap. 4 to start the ODF calculation.

7.2   Basis Functions of a 6-Point B-Spline

The basis functions for the 6-point B-spline are obtained from (3.3):

	$0 < u < 1$	$1 < u < 2$	$2 < u < 3$
N_{03}	$(1-u)^3$	0	0
N_{13}	$u(12-18u+7u^2)/4$	$(2-u)^3/4$	0
N_{23}	$u^2(18-11u)/12$	$(7u^3-36u^2$ $+54u-18)/12$	$(3-u)^3/6$
N_{33}	$u^3/6$	$(-7u^3+27u^2$ $-27u+9)/12$	$(3-u)^2(11u-15)/12$
N_{43}	0	$(u-1)^3/4$	$(3-u)(7u^2-24u+21)/4$
N_{53}	0	0	$(u-2)^3$

   As before, it is instructive to re-express these as linear combinations of Bernstein polynomials. We do this as follows: for each of the three segments, express the column vector $\{N_{i3}\}_{i=k}^{k+3}$ as a matrix product $\mathbf{Nu}$ where $\mathbf{u}$ is a column vector whose elements are $\mathbf{u}_i = u^i$ and $\mathbf{N}$ is a 4×4 constant matrix, and $k \in [0, 2]$. Note that the Bernstein polynomials, $B_{i3}(u - k)$, can be similarly expressed in the form $\mathbf{Bu}$, where $\mathbf{B}$ is a 4×4 constant matrix. Now rewrite the B-spline basis functions in the equivalent form $\mathbf{Nu} = \mathbf{NB}^{-1}\mathbf{Bu}$. Therefore the transform that converts the Bernstein polynomials into B-spline basis functions is $\mathbf{NB}^{-1}$. We find:

$$\begin{pmatrix} N_{03} \\ N_{13} \\ N_{23} \\ N_{33} \end{pmatrix} = \begin{pmatrix} 1 & 0 & 0 & 0 \\ 0 & 1 & \frac{1}{2} & \frac{1}{4} \\ 0 & 0 & \frac{1}{2} & \frac{7}{12} \\ 0 & 0 & 0 & \frac{1}{6} \end{pmatrix} \begin{pmatrix} B_{03}(u) \\ B_{13}(u) \\ B_{23}(u) \\ B_{33}(u) \end{pmatrix} \quad \text{for } 0 < u < 1 \quad (7.1)$$

$$\begin{pmatrix} N_{13} \\ N_{23} \\ N_{33} \\ N_{43} \end{pmatrix} = \begin{pmatrix} \frac{1}{4} & 0 & 0 & 0 \\ \frac{7}{12} & \frac{2}{3} & \frac{1}{3} & \frac{1}{6} \\ \frac{1}{6} & \frac{1}{3} & \frac{2}{3} & \frac{7}{12} \\ 0 & 0 & 0 & \frac{1}{4} \end{pmatrix} \begin{pmatrix} B_{03}(u-1) \\ B_{13}(u-1) \\ B_{23}(u-1) \\ B_{33}(u-1) \end{pmatrix} \quad \text{for } 1 < u < 2 \quad (7.2)$$

$$\begin{pmatrix} N_{23} \\ N_{33} \\ N_{43} \\ N_{53} \end{pmatrix} = \begin{pmatrix} \frac{1}{6} & 0 & 0 & 0 \\ \frac{7}{12} & \frac{1}{2} & 0 & 0 \\ \frac{1}{4} & \frac{1}{2} & 1 & 0 \\ 0 & 0 & 0 & 1 \end{pmatrix} \begin{pmatrix} B_{03}(u-2) \\ B_{13}(u-2) \\ B_{23}(u-2) \\ B_{33}(u-2) \end{pmatrix} \quad \text{for } 2 < u < 3. \quad (7.3)$$

We have computed these transforms simply for the purpose of confirming that they are consistent with the three-segment Bézier representation given below.

7.3 Decomposition into Three Bézier Segments

In order to represent this B-spline as three separate Bézier segments, for rendering purposes, we need to convert the knot vector from $U = (0\ 0\ 0\ 0\ 1\ 2\ 3\ 3\ 3\ 3)$ to $U = (0\ 0\ 0\ 0\ 1\ 1\ 1\ 1\ 2\ 2\ 2\ 2\ 3\ 3\ 3\ 3)$. To do so, we use (3.4) recursively to obtain a relationship between the six original B-spline control points $\mathbf{Q}$ and the 12 new Bézier control points $\mathbf{R}$:

$$\begin{pmatrix} \mathbf{R}_0 \\ \mathbf{R}_1 \\ \mathbf{R}_2 \\ \mathbf{R}_3 \\ \mathbf{R}_4 \\ \mathbf{R}_5 \\ \mathbf{R}_6 \\ \mathbf{R}_7 \\ \mathbf{R}_8 \\ \mathbf{R}_9 \\ \mathbf{R}_{10} \\ \mathbf{R}_{11} \end{pmatrix} = \begin{pmatrix} 1 & 0 & 0 & 0 & 0 & 0 \\ 0 & 1 & 0 & 0 & 0 & 0 \\ 0 & \frac{1}{2} & \frac{1}{2} & 0 & 0 & 0 \\ 0 & \frac{1}{4} & \frac{7}{12} & \frac{1}{6} & 0 & 0 \\ 0 & \frac{1}{4} & \frac{7}{12} & \frac{1}{6} & 0 & 0 \\ 0 & 0 & \frac{2}{3} & \frac{1}{3} & 0 & 0 \\ 0 & 0 & \frac{1}{3} & \frac{2}{3} & 0 & 0 \\ 0 & 0 & \frac{1}{6} & \frac{7}{12} & \frac{1}{4} & 0 \\ 0 & 0 & \frac{1}{6} & \frac{7}{12} & \frac{1}{4} & 0 \\ 0 & 0 & 0 & \frac{1}{2} & \frac{1}{2} & 0 \\ 0 & 0 & 0 & 0 & 1 & 0 \\ 0 & 0 & 0 & 0 & 0 & 1 \end{pmatrix} \begin{pmatrix} \mathbf{Q}_0 \\ \mathbf{Q}_1 \\ \mathbf{Q}_2 \\ \mathbf{Q}_3 \\ \mathbf{Q}_4 \\ \mathbf{Q}_5 \end{pmatrix}$$

Note that this transform is related to (7.1), (7.2) and (7.3) in the same way as noted in (6.5), which provides a link between a basis function transformation and the corresponding control point transformation.

7.4   ODF Results for a 6-Point B-Spline

Figure 7.1 shows the arm length for the 6-point B-spline. We see that there is only one main branch, as there was for the 5-point B-spline. The main difference is that the closed oval shape in Fig. 6.1 appears to have migrated from $c \approx 2$ to a location at $c \approx 18$ where it has partially merged with the S-shaped portion of the main branch in Fig. 7.1 to form a narrow isthmus, or avoided crossing, at $c = 18$, $a_1 = 10$. The previously minor glitch in Fig. 6.1 has thus been accentuated to be even more visible. We find once again that there is no smooth way to navigate between the two extreme kinds of behavior that the hypoTrochoid exhibits. For comparison purposes, the points $\mathbf{AB_1B_2CDE}$ are marked in Fig. 7.1, and correspond well to the same points in Fig. 6.1. Figure 7.2 shows the rms error for this spline. The 6-point B-spline is consistently better than the 5-point B-spline, by as little as a factor of 3 at $c = 20$, to as much as a factor of 6 at $c = 10$. As before, we note that the globally best solution is at $c \approx 1.3$, similar to the previous two fits. One new feature in Fig. 7.2 is that, at $c = 18.3$, the saddle point solution almost touches the local minimum solution. This feature also shows up in Fig. 7.1 as an avoided crossing in the arm lengths. It is interesting to see how this affects the lowest eigenvalue, shown in Fig. 7.3. This eigenvalue has a negative branch from $c = 17.8$ to 19.7, as expected for a saddle point; but it also has a very narrowly avoided crossing at $c = 18.3$ where the positive and negative branches almost touch. Comparing this to Figs. 4.5 and 5.1b we see the difference between a true crossing and an avoided crossing of solutions. The eigenvalues are shown in more detail in Fig. 7.4. This shows an avoided Type 2

Fig. 7.1 6-point B-spline arm length a_1

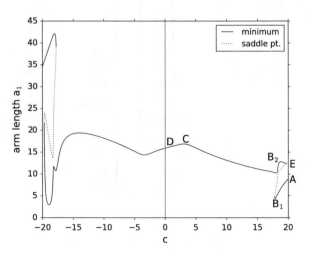

Fig. 7.2 6-point B-spline
rms error

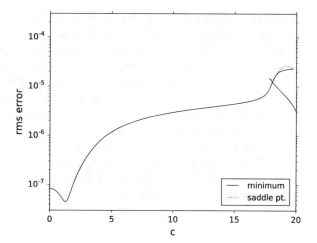

Fig. 7.3 6-point B-spline
lowest eigenvalue

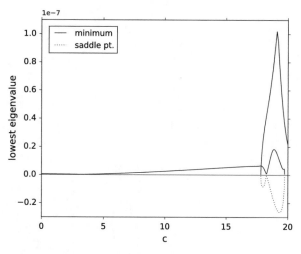

Fig. 7.4 6-point B-spline
eigenvalues of $\mathbf{M}$ and $\mathbf{M}^+$

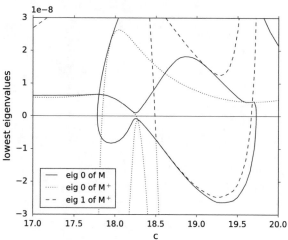

crossover of the lowest eigenvalue of $\mathbf{M}$, while the lowest eigenvalue of $\mathbf{M}^+$ has one branch that crosses zero and the other branch does not, confirming that this is not a true crossing. The second lowest eigenvalue of $\mathbf{M}^+$ is also shown since it experiences a narrowly avoided crossing with the lowest eigenvalue.

We note in conclusion that there is not much qualitative difference between the three fits performed so far. We have increased the number of degrees of freedom from 2 to 4, and then 6, without seeing any fundamental resolution of the problem of how to morph smoothly from a symmetric shape to an asymmetric shape. For this reason we now go further afield, to try a quartic Bézier curve. From a pragmatic point of view this may not be very useful because we have no way of easily rendering such a curve, but it will be interesting to see whether the higher degree curve is qualitatively better than a cubic spline.

Chapter 8
ODF Using a Quartic Bézier

The motivation for using a quartic Bézier is that the hypoTrochoid curve at $c = 20$ exhibits primarily quartic behavior at an endpoint due to the double inflection point. We will use a single quartic segment to try to produce a fit that is comparable in complexity to the 5-point B-spline. The Bézier basis functions are given by the Bernstein polynomials (3.2) with $p = 4$. There are 5 control points and 4 degrees of freedom in the fit. The knot vector is $U = (0\,0\,0\,0\,0\,1\,1\,1\,1\,1)$. The endpoints $\mathbf{Q}_0$ and $\mathbf{Q}_4$ will be the same as before, and the intermediate control points are given by

$$\mathbf{Q}_1 = (x_1, y_1) = (x_0 - a_1 \sin\theta_1,\, y_0 + a_1 \cos\theta_1)$$

$$\mathbf{Q}_2 = (x_2, y_2)$$

$$\mathbf{Q}_3 = (x_3, y_3) = (x_4 + a_2 \sin\theta_2,\, y_4 - a_2 \cos\theta_2).$$

The parameter vector is $\mathbf{a} \triangleq (a_1, a_2, x_2, y_2)$. The initial estimate of $\mathbf{a}$ will of course be different than it was for the B-spline case. The other notable difference is that (2.1) will now be septic in u, because $\mathbf{f}(u)$ is of degree 4 and $\mathbf{f}'(u)$ is of degree 3. However this is not a significant complication since we are using successive approximations in any event.

8.1 Initializing a Quartic Bézier

As before, we use a cubic Bézier to initialize the quartic calculation. Since both of these curves consist of a single segment, the initialization is somewhat simpler than it was for the B-splines previously used. We use a method called "Increasing the Degree of a Bézier Curve" [1, p. 213] to obtain this relationship between the quartic Bézier control points $\mathbf{Q}$ and the cubic Bézier control points $\mathbf{P}$:

A. Penner, *Fitting Splines to a Parametric Function*,
SpringerBriefs in Computer Science, https://doi.org/10.1007/978-3-030-12551-6_8

$$
\begin{pmatrix} \mathbf{Q}_0 \\ \mathbf{Q}_1 \\ \mathbf{Q}_2 \\ \mathbf{Q}_3 \\ \mathbf{Q}_4 \end{pmatrix} = \begin{pmatrix} 1 & 0 & 0 & 0 \\ \frac{1}{4} & \frac{3}{4} & 0 & 0 \\ 0 & \frac{1}{2} & \frac{1}{2} & 0 \\ 0 & 0 & \frac{3}{4} & \frac{1}{4} \\ 0 & 0 & 0 & 1 \end{pmatrix} \begin{pmatrix} \mathbf{P}_0 \\ \mathbf{P}_1 \\ \mathbf{P}_2 \\ \mathbf{P}_3 \end{pmatrix}
$$

Of course, we could also use (3.4) to obtain the same result using knot insertion, which would be somewhat more complicated. The above relationship between $\mathbf{P}$ and $\mathbf{Q}$ can be interpreted to mean that the (initial) quartic Bézier arm lengths a_1 and a_2 will be $\frac{3}{4}$ the cubic Bézier arm lengths, and that the new quartic Bézier control point $\mathbf{Q}_2$ will be the average of the cubic Bézier points $\mathbf{P}_1$ and $\mathbf{P}_2$. The change in arm lengths, in turn, can be rationalized as follows: assume that the cubic control points, $\mathbf{P}_i$, are equally spaced (either in x or y) with a spacing of 1. Then it can be seen, using the above equation, that the quartic control points, $\mathbf{Q}_i$, will also be equally spaced (in x or y) with a spacing of $\frac{3}{4}$. Equal spacing of control points is significant because it means that the relationship between x (or y) and u will be linear, which in turn means that the variable y (or x) is a polynomial in x (or y), which represents a considerable simplification. So if the original cubic Bézier was a polynomial then the quartic Bézier will also be a polynomial, as one might expect. It should be noted here that the same statement can also be made about the 5-point and 6-point B-spline initializations as well, but in those cases the demonstration is a bit more complicated because it involves multiplying, for example, (6.1) by (6.4) to confirm that the control points of the resulting two cubic Béziers are all equally spaced assuming that the original Bézier was a polynomial.

This gives us enough information to perform the ODF calculation. We do not need to worry about how to represent the results as cubic Béziers because that is not possible.

8.2   ODF Results for a Quartic Bézier

The ODF results for the quartic Bézier arm lengths and the rms error are shown in Figs. 8.1 and 8.2. The main new feature is that there are a large number of solutions and that some of them are incomplete. We will discuss this in Sect. 8.4. For now we focus on the branch that has the lowest error. This is a branch that starts at $(c = 20, a_1 = 26)$ and executes an S-shaped path to go through the middle point $(c = 0, a_1 = 35)$ and then the final point $(c = -20, a_1 = 42)$. This branch is also associated with an oval-shaped solution with limits $c = \pm 1.1$. The two solutions meet at $c = \pm 0.255$. Where they meet, we have used the augmented matrix $\mathbf{M}^+$ to show that the topology is identical to the behavior of the cubic Bézier at $c = 3.6$ (Sect. 5.2). This pair of solutions looks essentially the same as the cubic Bézier fit, except that the quartic S-shaped branch is upside down. The rms error associated with this solution is compared in Table 8.1 to the other fits performed so far: we see that

Fig. 8.1 Quartic Bézier arm length a_1

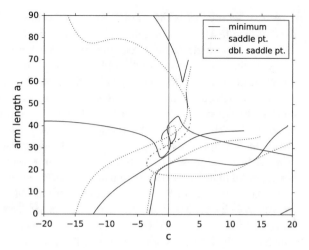

Fig. 8.2 Quartic Bézier rms error

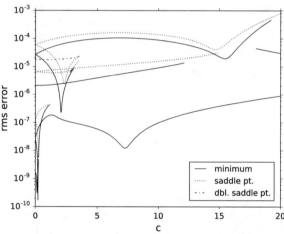

Table 8.1 rms error at $c = 0$ and $c = 20$

	d.f.	$c = 0$	$c = 20$
Cubic Bézier	2	2.0×10^{-6}	5.6×10^{-5}
5-point B-spline	4	3.9×10^{-7}	9.2×10^{-6}
6-point B-spline	6	8.2×10^{-8}	3.1×10^{-6}
Quartic Bézier	4	1.6×10^{-9}	9.0×10^{-7}
Beta2-spline	5	2.7×10^{-8}	5.9×10^{-6}
Beta1-spline	5	2.4×10^{-7}	9.3×10^{-7}

the quartic Bézier has the best fit by a significant margin even though it has fewer degrees of freedom than the 6-point B-spline. This is enough to justify the claim that the quartic component is doing a good job of emulating the double inflection point in the epiTrochoid. Unfortunately, this quartic shape is not directly supported by standard graphics API libraries, so the point is of mostly academic interest.

A new feature that is shown in these figures is the presence of a relatively short-lived branch that has two negative eigenvalues. We had previously seen numerous instances of a single negative eigenvalue, which we called saddle points, so we will call these new solutions "double saddle points" if they have two negative eigenvalues. The double saddle points might be viewed as being fairly unstable solutions which occur only locally. When they disappear, they will do so by merging with a single saddle point, in much the same way that a single saddle point will disappear by merging with a local minimum. The double saddle point branch will always have a higher rms error than its single saddle point counterpart, at least when they are near the point of coalescing, in the same way that a single saddle point always has a higher rms error than its local minimum counterpart.

We note also that in Fig. 8.2 the set of solutions can be roughly broken up into two distinct classes, based on rms error. There is the class consisting of an S-shaped branch and an oval-shaped branch, discussed above, and then there are "others", which have significantly higher rms error. The two classes even appear to be disjoint in that they do not seem to cross each other at any point in Fig. 8.2. This simplifies the analysis considerably. However, we still have the familiar problem that, if we wish to maintain continuity of rms error over the whole range of c, then it will be necessary to have a discontinuity in a_1 at the point $c = 0.45$, where we temporarily use the oval-shaped branch to form a bridge between two segments of the S-shaped branch.

8.3   Enumeration of Solutions

Since there are many solutions, it would be helpful if there were some way of knowing whether the set of solutions was complete. There is of course no way of knowing this, but there are some internal consistency tests which can be performed. First of all, at $c = 0$, we can classify the solutions as being either symmetric ($a_1 = a_2$) or asymmetric ($a_1 \neq a_2$). If they are symmetric they can exist by themselves, but if they are asymmetric they must occur in pairs since $a_2(c) = a_1(-c)$. A second test that can be performed concerns the relative number of saddle points and local minima. This relationship has been formally described in [3]. Here we present an intuitive interpretation of some of these ideas. If we consider a one-dimensional function which has unbounded maxima at either end, then it is clear that the number of internal local maxima will be one less than the number of local minima, assuming that we are not at a special location where two extrema have coalesced. In a multidimensional problem saddle points will play the role of local maxima. We note that solutions always disappear in pairs and that the pairs can consist of either a local minimum and a single saddle point, or a single saddle point and a double saddle point. (An alternative way of stating this is to say that the Morse indices will differ by 1, which corresponds to a single eigenvalue changing sign as we jump from one branch to the other.) Therefore we anticipate the following general rule:

$$local\_minima + double\_saddle\_points = single\_saddle\_points + 1 \qquad (8.1)$$

which we expect will be obeyed if no solutions have coalesced at this value of c. These two tests form a set of non-trivial criteria we can apply to any solution set in this work.

Equation (8.1) can be re-expressed in the language of graph theory. In Ref. [3] local minima/saddle points were associated with vertices/edges (V/E) in a connected graph. We can go one step farther and associate double saddle points with faces (F) of a polygon. If we restrict ourselves for the moment to a two-dimensional parameter space, then a double saddle point is actually a local maximum. In this case it is very easy to visualize how three saddle points could collaborate to form a triangle with local minima at the vertices, saddle points along the edges, and a single local maximum (double saddle point) in the middle of the triangle. It is also correspondingly difficult to imagine how a double saddle point could exist without having at least three saddle points around it to bring the function down locally before it finally rises to infinity as it eventually must. With this new association we can rewrite (8.1) as:

$$V + F = E + 1$$

which is just a re-statement of *Euler's characteristic* number for a planar object [4, p. 378], which is a polyhedron with one face removed. A similar interpretation, using the concepts of "source, saddle, and sink", is given in [5, Fig. 3–22, p. 149].

Applying these consistency criteria to the quartic Bézier solutions at $c = 0$ we get Table 8.2, where we have arranged the solutions according to rms error and have indicated the Morse index in each case. The solution set contains 3 unique symmetric and 10 asymmetric solutions, which occur in pairs, as expected. There are 6 local minima, 6 single saddle points and 1 double saddle point, which

Table 8.2 List of quartic Bézier solutions at $c = 0$

a_1	a_2	rms error	Morse index
35.5	35.5	1.6×10^{-9}	0
28.9	40.7	2.6×10^{-8}	0
40.7	28.9	2.6×10^{-8}	0
31.5	39.1	1.2×10^{-7}	1
39.1	31.5	1.2×10^{-7}	1
27.3	27.3	2.0×10^{-6}	0
23.0	35.2	6.5×10^{-6}	1
35.2	23.0	6.5×10^{-6}	1
31.4	31.4	1.7×10^{-5}	2
22.7	78.3	2.6×10^{-5}	0
78.3	22.7	2.6×10^{-5}	0
17.6	64.2	5.9×10^{-5}	1
64.2	17.6	5.9×10^{-5}	1

satisfies (8.1). Therefore we can at least claim that the solution set is internally consistent, even if we are not sure it is complete. This type of test has been very helpful when generating these results since otherwise it is not clear when to stop looking for new solutions. Generating new solutions is essentially a random process in which we deliberately choose inappropriate initial estimates for parameter values to see if there are any neighboring solutions we have missed.

8.4   Abnormal Truncation of Solutions

The above enumeration method is useful only in cases where no solutions have unexpectedly disappeared. Unfortunately, Fig. 8.1 shows a number of cases where solutions have terminated abnormally, due to convergence difficulties. This can occur for two reasons: problems in obtaining a unique value for $u(t)$, and negative arm lengths. We first discuss the problems that can occur in calculating $u(t)$. Figure 8.3 shows three examples of the function $u(t)$ at $c = 19.25$. At this value of c, Fig. 8.1 shows three solutions of interest: a local minimum at $a_1 = 27.0$, a saddle point at $a_1 = 31.7$, and another local minimum at $a_1 = 40.9$ which terminates abnormally. The local minimum at $a_1 = 27.0$ has a function $u(t)$ which is almost linear in Fig. 8.3, and this solution also has the lowest rms error (by a factor of about 600). The other two solutions for $u(t)$ both have inflection points near the midpoint of the range, and the solution which terminates abnormally ($a_1 = 40.9$) shows evidence of a very large slope in $u(t)$ at this point, which indicates that the calculation of $u(t)$ is almost indeterminate. If we pursue this calculation at higher values of c we find that the slope of $u(t)$ for this particular solution keeps on increasing until eventually the $u(t)$ curve becomes multivalued (S-shaped), in which case we have no strategy for how to proceed, namely which branch to use. In view of

Fig. 8.3 quartic Bézier $u(t)$ at $c = 19.25$

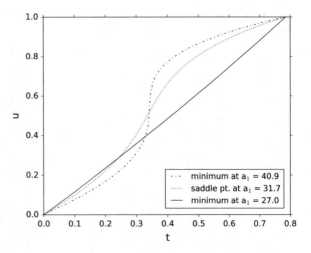

the fact that this particular solution has a very high rms error, the calculation of this branch was abandoned, since it was never intended that $u(t)$ should be multivalued.

A somewhat similar situation obtains when the arm lengths become negative. Figure 8.1 shows 10 instances in which solutions terminate abnormally due to an arm length approaching zero. These occur in five pairs which involve either a_1 or a_2. If an arm length is allowed to become negative, the corresponding spline will execute a very sharp turn near this endpoint so that the direction of motion rapidly reverses itself. This creates problems in the calculation of $u(t)$, since the hypoTrochoid curve does not have this behavior. With respect to endpoint conditions the following comment is intriguing [2, Sect. 3, p. 280]:

> As we are fitting a single Bézier segment the problem may be simplified, without loss of generality, by fixing the nodes associated with the first and last data points to occur at the ends of the curve segment, in particular we set $t_1 = 0$ and $t_m = 1$ respectively. This has the effect of preventing the curve segment from growing excessively outside the region of the data set. Although it does not force the endpoints of the curve segment to coincide with the first and last points of the data set, it does restrict them to be tangents to circles centered at these points.

This was probably not intended to be used in the context of negative arm lengths but it does raise an interesting possibility: one could possibly allow an arm length to become negative, if necessary, and then adjust the slope at the endpoint such that, at a certain non-zero value of u, the slope and direction of motion of the Bézier would become identical to the hypoTrochoid. The Bézier at this point would necessarily be displaced from the endpoint but would have the correct slope and we could have a one-to-one relationship between u and t from this point onwards. From a purely mathematical point of view this might be interesting to pursue, but we have chosen not to do so. First of all, there would be practical problems in determining exactly what the non-zero value of the offset in u would be; secondly, the rms error associated with this fit would likely be high due to the fact that the endpoints do not coincide. Rather than attempt such a solution, we will always terminate a branch at any time that an arm length becomes zero. Comparison of Figs. 8.1 and 8.2 shows that every abnormal termination of branches in these figures is associated with a solution that has an rms error sufficiently high as to exclude it from being of practical interest.

8.5 Topological Comparison of Béziers and B-Splines

In Sect. 8.2 it was noted that the quartic Bézier solution set consists of two disjoint sets of branches, one of which was not very interesting because of high rms error. Here we will focus on the two quartic Bézier branches that have the lowest error. However, our primary interest is not so much in the absolute error as in the ability to provide a smooth transition from one type of symmetry to another; so we are primarily interested in the topology of the solutions as a function of c. Figure 8.4 shows a comparison of the rms error for the cubic Bézier fit and the two best

Fig. 8.4 Compare cubic and quartic Bézier rms error

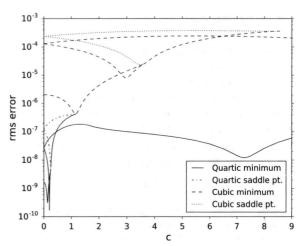

branches of the quartic Bézier fit. Apart from some scaling differences they are topologically identical. Viewed from this point of view, one could say that the quartic Bézier curve has not achieved the desired goal, which was to change the topology.

Performing a similar comparison (Figs. 6.2 and 7.2) of the two B-spline fits performed above, we find that they are also topologically essentially identical, and are distinctly different from either of the Bézier fits since they do not require any additional branches to serve as bridges between two limiting behaviors. Since the topology of the B-spline fits is much closer to the desired behavior than either of the Bézier fits, we will focus on them for the next two fitting trials. These two attempts will use Beta-splines which are essentially B-splines in which we relax the continuity requirements at the splice position.

References

1. R.H. Bartels, J.C. Beatty, B.A. Barsky, *An Introduction to Splines for Use in Computer Graphics & Geometric Modeling* (Morgan Kaufmann, Los Altos, 1987)
2. C.F. Borges, T.A. Pastva, Total least squares fitting of Bézier and B-Spline curves to ordered data. Comput. Aided Geom. Des. **19**, 275–289 (2002)
3. C.A. Floudas, H.T. Jongen, Global optimization: local minima and transition points. J. Global Optim. **32**, 409–415 (2005)
4. J.D. Foley, A. van Dam, S.K. Feiner, J.F. Hughes, R.L. Phillips, *Introduction to Computer Graphics* (Addison-Wesley, Reading, 1993)
5. V. Guillemin, A. Pollack, *Differential Topology* (Prentice-Hall, Englewood Cliffs, 1974)

Chapter 9
ODF Using a Beta2-Spline

Beta-splines have been developed [1, 2, 3, 5] as a result of the fact that the requirements of C^n continuity are overly restrictive when compared to what is visually observed. Visually, first order continuity is preserved if the slope dy/dx is continuous. This represents only one constraint at each breakpoint compared to C^1 continuity which requires that both x' and y' be continuous. Similarly, second order continuity is visually measured (4.2) by the curvature, κ, which represents only a single constraint at each breakpoint compared to C^2 continuity, which requires that both x'' and y'' be continuous. This has led to the concept of G^2 or *second degree geometric continuity* [2, p. 294], which the Beta-splines satisfy. These splines have two new degrees of freedom, called β_1 and β_2, at each breakpoint. The new parameters depend on the nature of the C^n continuity that is broken. β_1 is defined as follows [2, Eq. 14.2]:

$$\beta_1 \mathbf{f}'_{i-1}(1) = \mathbf{f}'_i(0) \tag{9.1}$$

where $\mathbf{f}'_i(0)$ is the first derivative of the position at the start of the ith segment and $\mathbf{f}'_{i-1}(1)$ is the same derivative at the end of the previous segment. β_1 is sometimes called *bias* [2, p. 306]. Setting $\beta_1 \neq 1$ breaks C^1 continuity and replaces it with G^1 continuity. This represents an asymmetric change in the relative Bézier arm lengths before and after a breakpoint.

The parameter β_2 is related to the curvature at the breakpoint. To impose G^2 continuity we first re-express (4.2) in vector notation:

$$\kappa_i(u) = (\mathbf{f}'_i(u) \times \mathbf{f}''_i(u))/|\mathbf{f}'_i(u)|^3$$

where the subscript i refers to the segment index. We wish to impose the constraint $\kappa_{i-1}(1) = \kappa_i(0)$. This can be re-expressed as:

© The Author(s), under exclusive license to Springer Nature Switzerland AG 2019
A. Penner, *Fitting Splines to a Parametric Function*,
SpringerBriefs in Computer Science, https://doi.org/10.1007/978-3-030-12551-6_9

$$\mathbf{f}'_{i-1}(1) \times \mathbf{f}''_{i-1}(1)/|\mathbf{f}'_{i-1}(1)|^3 = \mathbf{f}'_i(0) \times \mathbf{f}''_i(0)/|\mathbf{f}'_i(0)|^3$$

$$\mathbf{f}'_{i-1}(1) \times \mathbf{f}''_{i-1}(1)/|\mathbf{f}'_{i-1}(1)|^3 = \beta_1\mathbf{f}'_{i-1}(1) \times \mathbf{f}''_i(0)/(\beta_1^3|\mathbf{f}'_{i-1}(1)|^3)$$

$$\beta_1^2\mathbf{f}'_{i-1}(1) \times \mathbf{f}''_{i-1}(1) = \mathbf{f}'_{i-1}(1) \times \mathbf{f}''_i(0)$$

$$\mathbf{f}'_{i-1}(1) \times (\beta_1^2\mathbf{f}''_{i-1}(1) - \mathbf{f}''_i(0)) = 0$$

$$\therefore \beta_1^2\mathbf{f}''_{i-1}(1) - \mathbf{f}''_i(0) = -\beta_2\mathbf{f}'_{i-1}(1)$$

where we have used (9.1) and the fact that a cross product of a vector with itself is zero. This allowed us to introduce a new degree of freedom using the variable β_2, which can be rewritten as [2, Eq. 14.3]:

$$\beta_1^2\mathbf{f}''_{i-1}(1) + \beta_2\mathbf{f}'_{i-1}(1) = \mathbf{f}''_i(0). \tag{9.2}$$

β_2 is sometimes called *tension* [2, p. 307]. Setting $\beta_2 \neq 0$ breaks C^2 continuity and replaces it with G^2 continuity. We will show below that this represents a symmetric change in the Bézier arm lengths before and after a breakpoint. Collectively, the β parameters provide two extra degrees of freedom at each breakpoint, but we will study them separately since their symmetry properties are distinctly different and they each have unique characteristics when used in an ODF calculation. The Beta2-spline is the simpler of the pair, so we begin with it. This means setting $\beta_1 = 1$ and assuming C^1 continuity.

9.1   Rendering a Beta2-Spline

There are two different procedures that can be used when implementing these new spline functions. One method is to continue to use the same B-spline control points as before, but with a revised set of basis functions which depend on the β parameters [2]. This is the more general approach, suitable for splines with multiple breakpoints. An alternate method is to decompose the B-spline into separate Bézier segments and then manipulate the Bézier segments individually, with suitable constraints on the control arms to maintain the desired continuity. We will use this method since we have only one breakpoint, and two segments.

We begin with a 5-point B-spline, with control points $\mathbf{Q}_0 - \mathbf{Q}_4$; this is represented as two Bézier segments in Fig. 9.1, which is taken from Ref. [3, Fig. 3.3]. The relationship between the B-spline control points and the eight Bézier control points is given above (6.4), assuming that $\beta_1 = 1$ and $\beta_2 = 0$. If we know the B-spline control points we can calculate the following Bézier points: $\mathbf{R}_0 = \mathbf{Q}_0$, $\mathbf{R}_1 = \mathbf{Q}_1$, $\mathbf{R}_3 = \frac{1}{4}\mathbf{Q}_1 + \frac{1}{2}\mathbf{Q}_2 + \frac{1}{4}\mathbf{Q}_3$, $\mathbf{R}_6 = \mathbf{Q}_3$, and $\mathbf{R}_7 = \mathbf{Q}_4$. We will consider these five Bézier points to be known independent variables during the optimization process, in the sense that they are not dependent on β_1 or β_2. Since their relationship with $\mathbf{Q}_0 - \mathbf{Q}_4$ is invertible, we can use the 5-point B-spline as an initial estimate in the

ODF method, corresponding to $\beta_1 = 1$ and $\beta_2 = 0$. Now we need to determine the remaining three variables: $\mathbf{R}_2$, $\mathbf{R}_4$, and $\mathbf{R}_5$. When we impose C^0 continuity, the Bézier point $\mathbf{R}_4 = \mathbf{R}_3$ is also known, and is similarly independent of β_1 and β_2. We now wish to specify the two unknown points $\mathbf{R}_2$ and $\mathbf{R}_5$ using a combination of continuity constraints and β variables. These two points have 4 degrees of freedom, of which one will be an independent variable related to β_2, with $\beta_1 = 1$, and three will be determined by continuity.

In order to impose continuity constraints we need the following properties of the function:

$$\mathbf{f}_0'(1) = 3(\mathbf{R}_3 - \mathbf{R}_2) \qquad\qquad \mathbf{f}_1'(0) = 3(\mathbf{R}_5 - \mathbf{R}_4) \qquad\qquad (9.3)$$

$$\mathbf{f}_0''(1) = 6(\mathbf{R}_1 - 2\mathbf{R}_2 + \mathbf{R}_3) \qquad \mathbf{f}_1''(0) = 6(\mathbf{R}_4 - 2\mathbf{R}_5 + \mathbf{R}_6) \qquad (9.4)$$

Imposing C^1 continuity we get $\mathbf{R}_3 - \mathbf{R}_2 = \mathbf{R}_5 - \mathbf{R}_4$. This means that, not only are the points $\mathbf{R}_2$, $\mathbf{R}_3(= \mathbf{R}_4)$, and $\mathbf{R}_5$ collinear, but also the arm length $b_1 = b_2$ in Fig. 9.1. In the terminology of vector graphics programs such as Inkscape, this joint, or *node*, would be called both *smooth* and *symmetric*. We now have only two degrees of freedom left to determine, namely the angle ψ and the arm length $b \triangleq b_1 = b_2$, which we will refer to as just b from now on. We specify these variables using (9.2) with $\beta_1 = 1$:

$$\beta_2 \mathbf{f}_0'(1) = \mathbf{f}_1''(0) - \mathbf{f}_0''(1)$$

$$3\beta_2(\mathbf{R}_3 - \mathbf{R}_2) = 6(\mathbf{R}_4 - 2\mathbf{R}_5 + \mathbf{R}_6 - \mathbf{R}_1 + 2\mathbf{R}_2 - \mathbf{R}_3)$$

$$\beta_2(\mathbf{R}_3 - \mathbf{R}_2) = 2(-2\mathbf{R}_5 + \mathbf{R}_6 - \mathbf{R}_1 + 2\mathbf{R}_2)$$

$$\beta_2(\mathbf{R}_3 - \mathbf{R}_2) = 2(\mathbf{R}_6 - \mathbf{R}_1 - 2(\mathbf{R}_5 - \mathbf{R}_2))$$

$$\beta_2(\mathbf{R}_3 - \mathbf{R}_2) = 2(\mathbf{R}_6 - \mathbf{R}_1 - 2(\mathbf{R}_5 - \mathbf{R}_4 + \mathbf{R}_4 - \mathbf{R}_2))$$

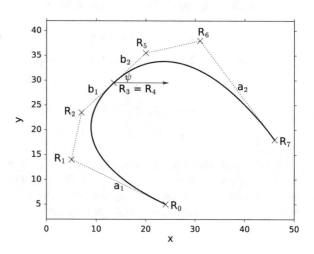

Fig. 9.1 Cubic Bézier control points for Beta-spline

$$\beta_2(\mathbf{R}_3 - \mathbf{R}_2) = 2(\mathbf{R}_6 - \mathbf{R}_1 - 2(\mathbf{R}_5 - \mathbf{R}_4 + \mathbf{R}_3 - \mathbf{R}_2))$$

$$\beta_2(\mathbf{R}_3 - \mathbf{R}_2) = 2(\mathbf{R}_6 - \mathbf{R}_1 - 4(\mathbf{R}_3 - \mathbf{R}_2))$$

$$(8 + \beta_2)(\mathbf{R}_3 - \mathbf{R}_2) = 2(\mathbf{R}_6 - \mathbf{R}_1)$$

$$\therefore (\mathbf{R}_3 - \mathbf{R}_2) \parallel (\mathbf{R}_6 - \mathbf{R}_1)$$

$$\text{and } (8 + \beta_2)|\mathbf{R}_3 - \mathbf{R}_2| = 2|\mathbf{R}_6 - \mathbf{R}_1|$$

$$(8 + \beta_2)b = 8b_0$$

$$\beta_2 = 8(b_0 - b)/b$$

where $b \triangleq |\mathbf{R}_3 - \mathbf{R}_2|$ and $b_0 \triangleq |\mathbf{R}_6 - \mathbf{R}_1|/4$. In this derivation we have used Eqs. (9.3) and (9.4) and the fact that $\mathbf{R}_3 - \mathbf{R}_2 = \mathbf{R}_5 - \mathbf{R}_4$ and $\mathbf{R}_3 = \mathbf{R}_4$. The final result is that $\mathbf{R}_3 - \mathbf{R}_2$ is parallel to $\mathbf{R}_6 - \mathbf{R}_1$, so the angle ψ is known in Fig. 9.1. Also, the arm length b is now directly related to β_2. We interpret this as follows: b is the actual arm length corresponding to a non-zero β_2, while b_0 corresponds to $\beta_2 = 0$. If we begin with a normal 5-point B-spline, and use (6.4) to convert it into a pair of Bézier segments, then the arm length, $|\mathbf{R}_3 - \mathbf{R}_2|$, will be b_0. Any deviation from this arm length will produce a non-zero β_2. Finally, if we constrain $b > 0$, as we always will, then we obtain the range $-8 < \beta_2 < \infty$. This range is a bit broader than that given in Ref. [5, p. 285], which suggested $0 \leq \beta_2$. (The theoretical reason for this constraint is not known.) It is also different from Ref. [4], which suggested $-4 < \beta_2$ (for $\beta_1 = 1$) based on keeping the basis functions positive. (However, this argument appears to be based on a spline which is not clamped, so it may not be applicable in our case.) In practice, the lowest (optimized) value we will see in this report is $\beta_2 \approx -1$ (Fig. 9.4), so we have not had occasion to determine which theoretical lower limit is most applicable.

We now have enough information to render the Beta2-spline. We use the notation $\mathbf{R}_0 - \mathbf{R}_7$ to refer to the Bézier control points. The endpoints $\mathbf{R}_0$ and $\mathbf{R}_7$ are fixed as usual, and the intermediate points are given by:

$$\mathbf{R}_1 = (x_1, y_1) = (x_0 - a_1 \sin \theta_1, y_0 + a_1 \cos \theta_1)$$

$$\mathbf{R}_2 = (x_2, y_2) = (x_3 - b \cos \psi, y_3 - b \sin \psi)$$

$$\mathbf{R}_3 = \mathbf{R}_4 = (x_3, y_3)$$

$$\mathbf{R}_5 = (x_5, y_5) = (x_3 + b \cos \psi, y_3 + b \sin \psi)$$

$$\mathbf{R}_6 = (x_6, y_6) = (x_7 + a_2 \sin \theta_2, y_7 - a_2 \cos \theta_2).$$

where ψ is calculated using the angle of $\mathbf{R}_6 - \mathbf{R}_1$. The parameter vector has five degrees of freedom: $\mathbf{a} \triangleq (a_1, a_2, x_3, y_3, b)$. We note in passing that the new variable ψ will introduce some nonlinearity into the calculation of the response function when we perform the ODF optimization, since ψ is a non-linear function of a_1 and a_2.

As expected, the initialization of the ODF calculation will proceed by first calculating the 5-point B-spline result; (6.4) is then used to calculate the initial Bézier control points $\mathbf{R}_i$. It is interesting to note that the arm lengths a_1 and a_2 are not changed by this conversion, but the midpoint $\mathbf{R}_3 (= \mathbf{R}_4)$ is redefined and the new arm length b is set equal to b_0.

9.2   Nonlinear Effects Due to ψ

The fact that ψ is dependent on both a_1 and a_2 will complicate the calculation of the response functions. First of all, in (2.3), when calculating $\partial u / \partial a_i$ we need to make the replacement:

$$d\mathbf{f}(u)/da_i = \partial \mathbf{f}(u)/\partial a_i + (\partial \psi / \partial a_i) \partial \mathbf{f}(u) / \partial \psi.$$

An analogous replacement also applies to the calculation of $d\mathbf{f}'(u)/da_i$. This needs to be done only for a_1 and a_2. The function $\partial \mathbf{f}(u)/\partial \psi$ is directly available from the definition of $\mathbf{R}_2$ and $\mathbf{R}_5$ above, while $\partial \psi / \partial a_i$ will be described below. Secondly, in the expression for G_{ij}, (2.8), we must compute the non-linear Hessian terms $\partial^2 \mathbf{f}(u)/\partial a_i \partial a_j$ for different combinations of the three variables a_1, a_2, and b. The calculation of $\partial^2 \mathbf{f}(u)/\partial a_1 \partial b$ and $\partial^2 \mathbf{f}(u)/\partial a_2 \partial b$ follows in a straightforward manner from the previous equation, but the calculation of $\partial^2 \mathbf{f}(u)/\partial a_i \partial a_j$, where $\{i, j\} \in \{1, 2\}$, requires the revised definition:

$$d^2\mathbf{f}(u)/da_i da_j = \partial^2 \mathbf{f}(u)/\partial \psi^2 (\partial \psi / \partial a_i)(\partial \psi / \partial a_j) + \partial \mathbf{f}(u)/\partial \psi (\partial^2 \psi / \partial a_i \partial a_j)$$

where we have used the fact that $\partial^2 \mathbf{f}(u)/\partial a_i \partial a_j = 0$. This will require us to evaluate $\partial^2 \mathbf{f}(u)/\partial \psi^2$, which follows directly from the definition of $\mathbf{R}_2$ and $\mathbf{R}_5$; and it will require the calculation of $\partial^2 \psi / \partial a_i \partial a_j$, which we will now describe. The angle ψ satisfies:

$$\tan \psi = \Delta y / \Delta x$$

where $\Delta y = y_6 - y_1$ and $\Delta x = x_6 - x_1$. Therefore

$$d\psi / da_i = (-\Delta x \cos \theta_i - \Delta y \sin \theta_i)/((\Delta x)^2 + (\Delta y)^2)$$

where $i \in \{1, 2\}$. Taking another derivative, we find:

$$d^2\psi / da_i da_j = \frac{((\Delta x)^2 - (\Delta y)^2) \sin(\theta_i + \theta_j) - 2\Delta x \Delta y \cos(\theta_i + \theta_j)}{((\Delta x)^2 + (\Delta y)^2)^2}$$

where $\{i, j\} \in \{1, 2\}$.

9.3   Continuity of the Beta2-Spline Integrands

The Beta2-spline introduces a new, and unwelcome, possibility that the integrands encountered in the calculation of the response functions may be discontinuous. This could significantly complicate the numerical integrations in (2.2) and (2.5). The potential discontinuity can be analytically described by (9.1), which states that $\mathbf{f}'(u)$ is continuous, while (9.2) indicates that $\mathbf{f}''(u)$ is not, for $\beta_1 = 1$. To see what impact this has on the integrands, we begin with the fact that the right hand side of (2.3) is continuous, since it contains only $\mathbf{f}'(u)$. Therefore, if we can prove that $E(u)$ is continuous, then so will be the functions $\partial u / \partial a_i$, which would give us the desired level of continuity in (2.2), (2.7), and (2.8). Rewriting (2.4), and using (9.2) to calculate the difference at $u = 1$, we see that $E(u)$ will be incremented by an amount

$$\Delta E(1) = 0 + \beta_2 f_x'(1)(f_x(1) - g_x(t))$$
$$+ 0 + \beta_2 f_y'(1)(f_y(1) - g_y(t)).$$

Therefore, after invoking (2.1) yet again, we get the desired continuity.

9.4   ODF Results for a Beta2-Spline

The ODF results for the Beta2-spline arm lengths and the rms error are shown in Figs. 9.2 and 9.3. The corresponding value of β_2 is shown in Fig. 9.4. Since this function is symmetric in c, only the positive half is shown. The arm length results show a lot of complexity, similar to the quartic Bézier results. Not only are there a lot of solutions, but also there are two branches that temporarily have double

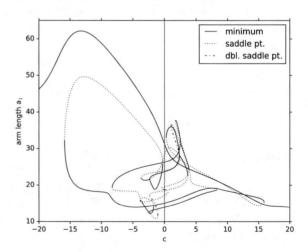

Fig. 9.2 Beta2-spline arm length a_1

Fig. 9.3 Beta2-spline rms error

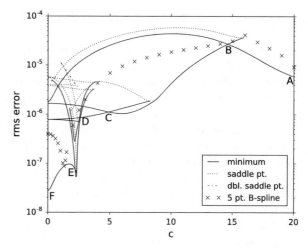

Fig. 9.4 Beta2-spline value of β_2

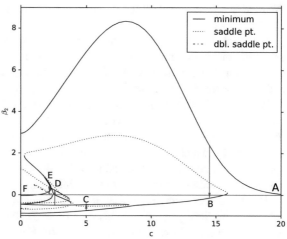

saddle points. In addition, there are a number of instances of what appear to be avoided crossings of solutions. However, there is one encouraging feature: namely, a complete lack of abnormal terminations of solutions due to negative arm lengths or non-unique relationships between u and t. The level of complexity, compared to the 5-point B-spline, is a bit surprising given that we have added only a single degree of freedom (β_2). There are also a number of instances where there are pairs of solutions that seem to run parallel to each other over large ranges. For example, in Fig. 9.2 the arm length goes through a complete reversal at ($c = 16, a_1 = 15$) and another partial reversal at ($c = 8, a_1 = 18$). Similarly, in Fig. 9.4 there is a pair of solutions parallel to each other with $\beta_2 \approx -\frac{1}{2}$ and $4 < c < 8$, with one solution being a local minimum while the other is a saddle point. These pairs of solutions often look very similar when viewed as arm length or as β_2, but may look very different when we view the corresponding rms error in Fig. 9.3, since one branch is a saddle point while the other is a local minimum. When they meet each other, they will typically annihilate in a Type 1 merge.

A new feature of the Beta2-spline results is that there is a single solution branch that runs all the way from $c = 20$ to $c = -20$ with no breaks, and with no multiple solutions at any point. This is seen most easily in the β_2 plot in Fig. 9.4. The Beta2-spline fit is unique in this respect, since it is the only one we have seen so far that is able to continuously morph from one extreme to the other. This branch has a β_2 value that is significantly higher than the other branches, corresponding to a high *tension*. High *tension* typically means [2, p.307] that the spline curve will be pulled closer to the B-spline control points than otherwise. This also corresponds to a decreased value of b relative to b_0, which is normally associated with higher local curvature. Unfortunately this continuous branch is not of much practical help since the rms error associated with it is fairly high. For $c < 15$ there are other branches that have significantly lower rms error, and typically these branches are associated with negative β_2, meaning lower than normal tension, or larger arm length ($b > b_0$). We note that $\beta_2 > -1$ at all times, so we are not close to the theoretical lower limit of -8.

We check the internal consistency of the set of solutions as follows: at $c = 0$ there are a total of 11 solutions, of which 5 are symmetric and 6 are asymmetric solutions which occur in pairs as expected. There are 5 local minima, 1 double saddle point, and 5 single saddle points, which is consistent with (8.1).

It is interesting to note that the minimum error solution is typically associated with fairly small β_2. At $c = 20$ we find $\beta_2 = 0.05$ and at $c = 0$ the global minimum in error occurs with $\beta_2 = -0.04$. It is also worth noting that the Beta2-spline is the only curve for which the global minimum error occurs at $c = 0$. For the 5-point B-spline it occurred at $c \approx 1.2$ and all the other fits also had this minimum at non-zero c, including the Beta1-spline in Chap. 10. It appears that the extra degree of freedom, b, which is a symmetric expansion of the arm length, was very helpful for the case where we are fitting a circle. In this case ($c = 0$), Table 8.1 shows that the Beta2-spline is second only to the quartic Bézier fit. For comparison purposes, Fig. 9.3 shows some values of the rms error for the 5-point B-spline, plotted as crosses. There are two cases for which the two sets of curves appear to touch each other. One case is at $c = 16$ where the B-spline makes a discontinuous jump across an S-shaped branch while the Beta2-spline experiences a coalescing of two solutions. The other case is at $c \approx 1.2$ where the B-spline has a global minimum. Other than these two cases, the Beta2-spline rms error is significantly better than the 5-point B-spline, so one might conclude that the extra effort was justified.

Finally, we address the primary reason for performing this fit, namely continuity of the optimum solution. In Fig. 9.3, if we wish to follow the path of minimum rms error, we have to follow the points ABCDEF, which switch branches at $c = 14.5$, 5.0, 2.6, and 2.2. These switches are continuous in the rms error, but in Figs. 9.4 and 9.5 they represent discontinuous jumps in β_2 and a_1, which are shown as arrows. The jump at $c = 14.5$ serves essentially the same purpose as the corresponding jump in the 5-point B-spline fit at $c = 16$, while the large jump in a_1 at $c = 2.6$ is reminiscent of the large change required in the original cubic Bézier fit at $c = 3.6$ in

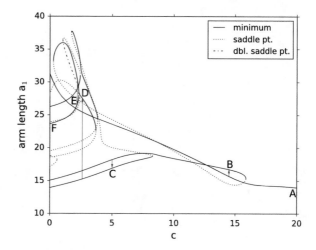

Fig. 9.5 Beta2-spline arm length a_1 transitions

Fig. 4.3. In any event, this does not achieve the desired goal of a single, continuously variable, optimum solution.

References

1. B.A. Barsky, A.D. DeRose, The beta2-spline: a special case of the beta-spline curve and surface representation. IEEE Comput. Graph. **5**(9), 46–58 (1985)
2. R.H. Bartels, J.C. Beatty, B.A. Barsky, *An Introduction to Splines for Use in Computer Graphics & Geometric Modeling* (Morgan Kaufmann, Los Altos, 1987)
3. A.D. DeRose, *Geometric Continuity: A Parametrization Independent Measure of Continuity for Computer Aided Geometric Design*. Ph.D. Thesis, University of California, Berkeley (1985)
4. F. De Tisi, M. Rossini, Behavior of the beta-splines with values of the parameters beta2 negative. Comput. Aided Geom. Des. **9**, 419–423 (1992)
5. P. Dierckx, B. Tytgat, Generating the Bézier points of a β-spline curve. Comput. Aided Geom. Des. **6**, 279–291 (1989)

Chapter 10
ODF Using a Beta1-Spline

The Beta1-spline is perhaps the most challenging curve used here, since it has the lowest degree of continuity, so much so that it is not always immediately obvious whether the integrands in (2.2) and (2.5) are continuous or not (Sect. 10.3). It is similar to the Beta2-spline except that the node at the Bézier join is only *smooth*, not *symmetric*. We will use the notation of Fig. 9.1 and the analytical definitions in (9.1) and (9.2), with $\beta_2 = 0$, to develop the description of the spline.

10.1 Rendering a Beta1-Spline

Begin by considering $\{\mathbf{R}_0, \mathbf{R}_1, \mathbf{R}_3 = \mathbf{R}_4, \mathbf{R}_6, \mathbf{R}_7\}$ as independent variables, which leaves $\mathbf{R}_2$ and $\mathbf{R}_5$ to be determined. Now define $\beta_1 \neq 1$ using (9.1). This establishes that $\mathbf{R}_2, \mathbf{R}_3 = \mathbf{R}_4$, and $\mathbf{R}_5$ are collinear, and it defines the arm length ratio $b_2/b_1 \triangleq \beta_1$. This leaves only two variables unspecified, namely ψ and the arm length b_1 (or b_2). We evaluate them by implementing (9.2) with $\beta_2 = 0$:

$$\beta_1^2 \mathbf{f}_0''(1) = \mathbf{f}_1''(0)$$

$$\beta_1^2 (\mathbf{R}_1 - 2\mathbf{R}_2 + \mathbf{R}_3) = \mathbf{R}_4 - 2\mathbf{R}_5 + \mathbf{R}_6$$

$$\beta_1^2 (2(\mathbf{R}_3 - \mathbf{R}_2) - (\mathbf{R}_3 - \mathbf{R}_1)) = \mathbf{R}_6 - \mathbf{R}_4 - 2(\mathbf{R}_5 - \mathbf{R}_4)$$

$$\beta_1^2 (2(\mathbf{R}_3 - \mathbf{R}_2) - (\mathbf{R}_3 - \mathbf{R}_1)) = \mathbf{R}_6 - \mathbf{R}_4 - 2\beta_1 (\mathbf{R}_3 - \mathbf{R}_2)$$

$$(2\beta_1^2 + 2\beta_1)(\mathbf{R}_3 - \mathbf{R}_2) = \mathbf{R}_6 - \mathbf{R}_4 + \beta_1^2 (\mathbf{R}_3 - \mathbf{R}_1)$$

$$\mathbf{R}_3 - \mathbf{R}_2 = \frac{\beta_1^2 (\mathbf{R}_3 - \mathbf{R}_1) + \mathbf{R}_6 - \mathbf{R}_4}{2\beta_1 (1 + \beta_1)}$$

© The Author(s), under exclusive license to Springer Nature Switzerland AG 2019
A. Penner, *Fitting Splines to a Parametric Function*,
SpringerBriefs in Computer Science, https://doi.org/10.1007/978-3-030-12551-6_10

$$\therefore (\mathbf{R}_3 - \mathbf{R}_2) \parallel \beta_1^2(\mathbf{R}_3 - \mathbf{R}_1) + \mathbf{R}_6 - \mathbf{R}_4$$

$$\text{and } b_1 = \frac{|\beta_1^2(\mathbf{R}_3 - \mathbf{R}_1) + \mathbf{R}_6 - \mathbf{R}_4|}{2\beta_1(1 + \beta_1)}$$

This allows us to calculate ψ (the angle of $\mathbf{R}_3 - \mathbf{R}_2$), and it also allows us to relate b_1 to β_1, so the spline is completely specified.

To render the Beta1-spline we use the notation $\mathbf{R}_0 - \mathbf{R}_7$ to refer to the Bézier control points. The endpoints $\mathbf{R}_0$ and $\mathbf{R}_7$ are fixed as usual, and the intermediate points are given by:

$$\mathbf{R}_1 = (x_1, y_1) = (x_0 - a_1 \sin\theta_1, y_0 + a_1 \cos\theta_1)$$
$$\mathbf{R}_2 = (x_2, y_2) = (x_3 - b_1 \cos\psi, y_3 - b_1 \sin\psi)$$
$$\mathbf{R}_3 = \mathbf{R}_4 = (x_3, y_3)$$
$$\mathbf{R}_5 = (x_5, y_5) = (x_3 + b_2 \cos\psi, y_3 + b_2 \sin\psi)$$
$$\mathbf{R}_6 = (x_6, y_6) = (x_7 + a_2 \sin\theta_2, y_7 - a_2 \cos\theta_2).$$

where ψ is calculated using the angle of $\beta_1^2(\mathbf{R}_3 - \mathbf{R}_1) + \mathbf{R}_6 - \mathbf{R}_4$. The parameter vector has five degrees of freedom: $\mathbf{a} \triangleq (a_1, a_2, x_3, y_3, \beta_1)$. We note that the new variable β_1 will introduce some nonlinearity into the calculation of the response function when we perform the ODF optimization, since ψ, b_1, and b_2 are non-linear functions of β_1.

As before, the initialization of the ODF calculation will proceed by first calculating the 5-point B-spline result, and using it to define the initial Bézier control points $\mathbf{R}_i$, with the initial estimate $\beta_1 = 1$.

10.2   Nonlinear Effects Due to β_1

When calculating $\partial u / \partial a_i$ in (2.3) we will need to evaluate the first order response functions $d\mathbf{f}(u)/da_i$, subject to the internal constraints. The constraints can be summarized as follows:

$$\mathbf{R}_5 - \mathbf{R}_3 = \beta_1(\mathbf{R}_3 - \mathbf{R}_2)$$

$$\mathbf{R}_3 - \mathbf{R}_2 = \frac{\beta_1^2(\mathbf{R}_3 - \mathbf{R}_1) + \mathbf{R}_6 - \mathbf{R}_3}{2\beta_1(1 + \beta_1)}.$$

In these equations, we view $\mathbf{R}_1$, $\mathbf{R}_3$ and $\mathbf{R}_6$ as independent variables, while $\mathbf{R}_2$ and $\mathbf{R}_5$ are dependent. We evaluate the constrained response using the $\mathbf{R}_i$ variables, with the understanding that when we implement the numerical calculations, we will convert them in a straightforward manner to the variables of $\mathbf{a}$, since $\mathbf{R}_1$ ($\mathbf{R}_6$) is linearly related to a_1 (a_2) and $\mathbf{R}_3 = (x_3, y_3)$. Therefore the constrained responses are:

	for $0 < u < 1$	for $1 < u < 2$
$d\mathbf{f}/d\mathbf{R}_1 =$	$\partial\mathbf{f}/\partial\mathbf{R}_1 + (\partial\mathbf{f}/\partial\mathbf{R}_2)\partial\mathbf{R}_2/\partial\mathbf{R}_1$	$0 + (\partial\mathbf{f}/\partial\mathbf{R}_5)\partial\mathbf{R}_5/\partial\mathbf{R}_1$
$d\mathbf{f}/d\mathbf{R}_6 =$	$0 + (\partial\mathbf{f}/\partial\mathbf{R}_2)\partial\mathbf{R}_2/\partial\mathbf{R}_6$	$\partial\mathbf{f}/\partial\mathbf{R}_6 + (\partial\mathbf{f}/\partial\mathbf{R}_5)\partial\mathbf{R}_5/\partial\mathbf{R}_6$
$d\mathbf{f}/d\mathbf{R}_3 =$	$\partial\mathbf{f}/\partial\mathbf{R}_3 + (\partial\mathbf{f}/\partial\mathbf{R}_2)\partial\mathbf{R}_2/\partial\mathbf{R}_3$	$\partial\mathbf{f}/\partial\mathbf{R}_3 + (\partial\mathbf{f}/\partial\mathbf{R}_5)\partial\mathbf{R}_5/\partial\mathbf{R}_3$
$d\mathbf{f}/d\beta_1 =$	$0 + (\partial\mathbf{f}/\partial\mathbf{R}_2)\partial\mathbf{R}_2/\partial\beta_1$	$0 + (\partial\mathbf{f}/\partial\mathbf{R}_5)\partial\mathbf{R}_5/\partial\beta_1$

where

$$\partial\mathbf{R}_2/\partial\mathbf{R}_1 = \beta_1/2(1+\beta_1) \quad \bigg| \quad \partial\mathbf{R}_5/\partial\mathbf{R}_1 = -\beta_1^2/2(1+\beta_1)$$
$$\partial\mathbf{R}_2/\partial\mathbf{R}_6 = -1/2\beta_1(1+\beta_1) \, \bigg| \, \partial\mathbf{R}_5/\partial\mathbf{R}_6 = 1/2(1+\beta_1)$$
$$\partial\mathbf{R}_2/\partial\mathbf{R}_3 = (1+\beta_1)/2\beta_1 \quad \bigg| \quad \partial\mathbf{R}_5/\partial\mathbf{R}_3 = (1+\beta_1)/2$$

and

$$\beta_1(1+\beta_1)\partial\mathbf{R}_2/\partial\beta_1 = -\beta_1(\mathbf{R}_3 - \mathbf{R}_1) + (1+2\beta_1)(\mathbf{R}_3 - \mathbf{R}_2)$$

$$(1+\beta_1)\partial\mathbf{R}_5/\partial\beta_1 = \beta_1(\mathbf{R}_3 - \mathbf{R}_1) - (\mathbf{R}_5 - \mathbf{R}_3)$$

Note that the same formulas will also apply if we replace $\mathbf{f}(u)$ with $\mathbf{f}'(u)$.

The remaining issue is the calculation of the Hessian terms $d^2\mathbf{f}(u)/da_i da_j$. We note that the only non-zero Hessian terms are of the type $d^2\mathbf{f}(u)/d\mathbf{R}_i d\beta_1$ and $d^2\mathbf{f}(u)/d\beta_1^2$, where $i \in \{1, 3, 6\}$. Since terms of the type $\partial\mathbf{f}/\partial\mathbf{R}_i$ are always constant, therefore the Hessian terms can be evaluated by taking another derivative with respect to β_1 in the above expressions for $\partial\mathbf{R}_2/\partial x$ and $\partial\mathbf{R}_5/\partial x$ where $x \in \{\mathbf{R}_1, \mathbf{R}_6, \mathbf{R}_3, \beta_1\}$.

10.3   Continuity of the Beta1-Spline Integrands

Similarly to the Beta2-spline, the Beta1-spline also introduces the possibility that the integrands in the calculation of the response functions may be discontinuous. This time the discontinuities are a bit more obvious. Figure 10.1 shows the functions $\mathbf{f}'(u)$ and $\mathbf{f}''(u)$ for a non-optimized calculation at $c = 10$ and $(a_1, a_2, x_3, y_3, \beta_1) = (25, 30, 166, 68, 1.5)$. We see that all four functions are discontinuous at $u = 1$, and not by the same ratio in all cases. This could significantly complicate the numerical integrations in (2.2) and (2.5). The discontinuity can be analytically predicted by (9.1), which states that the function $\mathbf{f}'(u)$ will be instantaneously scaled by a factor β_1 at $u = 1$, and by (9.2), which states that $\mathbf{f}''(u)$ will be scaled by a factor β_1^2 at the same time, if $\beta_2 = 0$. Both of these predictions are consistent with Fig. 10.1.

Figure 10.2 shows the corresponding functions $\partial u/\partial a_i$ for this run. These functions are also discontinuous at $u = 1$, but in the opposite direction (the magnitude of each function decreases instead of increasing). In this figure the function $\partial u/\partial\beta_1$

Fig. 10.1 $\mathbf{f}'(u)$ and $\mathbf{f}''(u)$ for a Beta1-spline

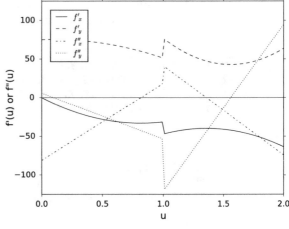

Fig. 10.2 $\partial u/\partial a_i$ for a Beta1-spline

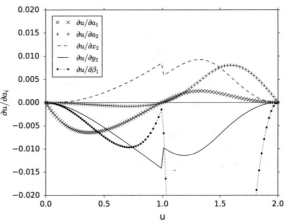

is unique in that it appears to show a zero at $u = 1$. The other four functions show a discontinuity; the different response is presumably related to the fact that their independent variables have dimensions of length while β_1 is dimensionless. The nature of the discontinuity can be predicted by (2.3). The right hand side in this equation is proportional to $\mathbf{f}'(u)$, so it scales as the factor β_1 at $u = 1$, while the left hand side, $E(u)$, is proportional to $\mathbf{f}''(u)$ so it scales as β_1^2 at the same time. As a result, $\partial u/\partial a_i$ will scale by the factor $1/\beta_1$ at $u = 1$, which is consistent with Fig. 10.2.

The net result of these two effects is that there will be no discontinuity in the integrands. In (2.2), (2.7) and (2.8) the number of times that u appears in the numerator always agrees with the number of appearances in the denominator. This is required by dimensional consistency in u, and ensures that the discontinuous scale factors will always cancel at $u = 1$, so that we can perform a numerical integration by treating these functions as being continuous. The only remaining disturbing feature of these figures is that we have not captured the zero in $\partial u/\partial \beta_1$ very accurately at

$u = 1$, since we are moving in constant increments of the variable t, not u, so the calculation was not performed at precisely $u = 1$. However, this inaccuracy is caused by a discontinuity of a higher order (in the slope of $\partial u / \partial \beta_1$, not the value), which can be easily remedied by using a higher N value, or by performing an interpolation of an additional data point in order to estimate more precisely the t value that yields $u = 1$.

10.4 ODF Results for a Beta1-Spline

The ODF results for the Beta1-spline arm lengths and rms error are shown in Figs. 10.3 and 10.4. We see that the solution set is even more complex than it was for the Beta2-spline, with three solutions at $c = 20$ (two local minima and a saddle point)

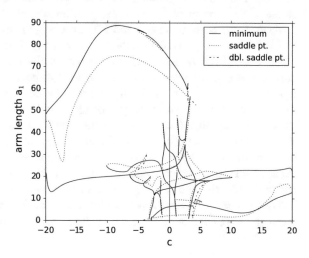

Fig. 10.3 Beta1-spline arm length a_1

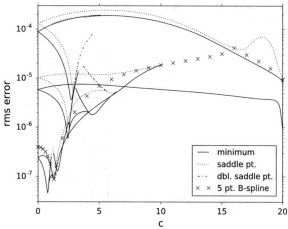

Fig. 10.4 Beta1-spline rms error

instead of the normal single solution. At $c = 0$ it has the same total number, 11, as the Beta2-spline, of which 5 are saddle points and 6 are local minima, so we again satisfy the expected rules concerning internal consistency. There is a difference in the amount of symmetry, however: the Beta2-spline had 5 symmetric solutions at $c = 0$, while the Beta1-spline has only one symmetric solution. This solution has $\beta_1 = 1$, so it is identical to the corresponding 5-point B-spline solution at $c = 0$. With respect to β_1 we have the following transform behavior: changing the sign of c is equivalent to interchanging the start point and end point of the hypoTrochoid curve, so β_1 will follow the rule: $\beta_1(-c) = 1/\beta_1(c)$. In Fig. 10.5 we have plotted β_1 on a logarithmic scale, showing only the positive range of c, since the function $log(\beta_1)$ is anti-symmetric in c.

Comparing the Beta1-spline and the 5-point B-spline at $c = 20$ we see that the Beta1-spline has a solution with $\beta_1 = 1.08$ at $c = 20$ which has an rms error very close to the corresponding B-spline result. However, this is not the optimum solution: this occurs at $\beta_1 = 0.21$, with an rms error that is almost 10 times lower than the B-spline result, and is almost as good as the quartic Bézier result (Table 8.1). In this particular fit, the low β_1 value leads to a result in which the four Bézier control points, $\mathbf{R}_4 - \mathbf{R}_7$, are almost equally spaced in a region where the curvature is extremely low due to the double inflection point at $\mathbf{R}_7$. This is clearly a desirable result, and is made possible only by the asymmetry introduced by β_1. This type of solution remains very good all the way down to $c = 7$, with a β_1 value consistently less than 0.4. It is also better than the Beta2-spline result for $c > 10$. The fact that the Beta1-spline does well in this range of c does not come as any surprise: since the object we are fitting is highly asymmetric for $c > 10$, it is to be expected that an asymmetric degree of freedom like β_1 will outperform a symmetric parameter like β_2. At $c = 0$ the situation is reversed: the β_1 spline has a symmetric solution ($\beta_1 = 1$, $a_1 = a_2$) which is identical to the corresponding 5-point B-spline result at $c = 0$, but this solution is a saddle point in the Beta1-spline solution space

Fig. 10.5 Beta1-spline value of β_1

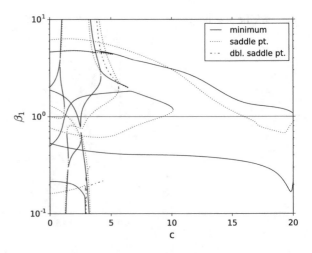

while it was a local minimum in the B-spline case. As a result, it has two slightly better asymmetric neighbors with $\beta_1 = 0.497$ and 2.01. Neither of these, however, is as good as the best Beta2-spline solution at $c = 0$, which is the best cubic spline result of all. (See Table 8.1 in Sect. 8.2)

The Beta1-spline shows a number of features familiar from the Beta2-spline, namely pairs of solutions that run parallel to each other over a large range of c and then self-annihilate. There are also two instances of temporary branches that are double saddle-points. Apart from this, it is the most attractive solution in the sense that it provides a smooth path for all $c > 10$, with no branch switching required, which neither the 5-point, nor the 6-point B-spline, nor the Beta2-spline can do. One can attribute this flexibility to the fact that β_1 can emulate different levels of asymmetry at the breakpoint $u = 1$, which the other curves cannot. However, in order to achieve optimum rms error as we move from $c = 20$ to $c = 0$, it is still necessary to make at least two jumps between branches, at $c = 7$ and $c = 1.2$. Also, this particular spline presents us with some unique numerical challenges, to be described below.

10.5   Numerical Problems with the Beta1-Spline

We recall that, in the quartic Bézier fit, there were cases where the solution would terminate abnormally, usually due to some well-defined reason such as an arm length approaching zero. The Beta1-spline also exhibits a number of such abnormal terminations, where it becomes increasingly difficult to converge to a solution. In this case, however, the abnormal terminations are more complex than before. Some of these are highlighted in Fig. 10.6, where they have been assigned numbers according to the following classification scheme:

Fig. 10.6 Classification of Beta1-spline terminations

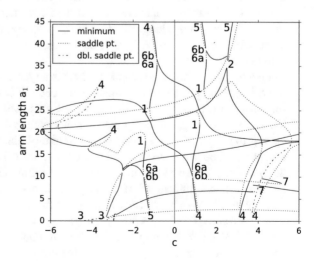

1. *Normal coalescence of two solutions (Type 1 merge)*. These have the same general appearance as such coalescing behavior in previous fits. The ones highlighted here are of the type where a local minimum coalesces with a saddle point.

2. *Closely avoided crossings*. These are not abnormal terminations but they represent cases where it was necessary to increment c in very small steps due to the extreme curvature at the avoided crossing. This particular avoided crossing is more complex than any previously encountered since it contains three or four branches instead of the normal two.

3. $a_1 = 0$ *at negative c*. This type of abort is typical of what the quartic Bézier showed in Fig. 8.1. The two instances shown here have $c = -4.45$ and -3.315 when a_1 crosses zero, while $\beta_1 = 0.22$ and 0.31, respectively. Both β_1 values are in the range of what we would consider to be "normal". These terminations are qualitatively the same as what we have seen previously, but we report them as a distinct case because they are different from cases 4 and 5, below.

4. $a_1 \rightarrow 0$ *and* $\beta_1 \rightarrow \infty$ *at positive c*. When a_1 approaches zero at positive c, we are not able to approach the zero very closely. We encounter convergence difficulties when $a_1 \approx 2$ or 3. This particular problem never occurred before. It is apparently caused by the fact that β_1 is simultaneously increasing without limit, which can be seen in Fig. 10.5 at $c = 3.1$ and 3.7. In the terminology of Fig. 9.1, the arm lengths a_1 and b_1 in the first Bézier segment are almost equal and are both approaching zero, while b_2 in the second Bézier segment becomes inversely large. The increase in b_2 will affect the curvature at the endpoint $\mathbf{R}_7$. This will lead to an ill-conditioned problem since a small change in a_1 at the start point $\mathbf{R}_0$ may have a large effect on the curvature at the endpoint $\mathbf{R}_7$. At the same time, the lowest eigenvalue of the $\mathbf{M}$ matrix is approaching zero in this limit, which will lead to instability. In any event, we were not able to approach this limit nearly as closely as one might hope.

5. *Large* $a_1, a_2 \rightarrow 0$, *and* $\beta_1 \rightarrow 0$ *at positive c*. These solutions are complementary to Case 4, with the roles of the two Bézier segments interchanged. A small change in $a_2 \approx b_2$ will have a large effect on the curvature at the start point, leading to an unstable situation. As in Case 4, the lowest eigenvalue of $\mathbf{M}$ is approaching zero in this limit.

6. *Compound merges/avoided crossings*. This is a type of event never seen before. In each case it consists of a normal coalescence of two solutions (at point **6a**) followed closely by an avoided crossing (at point **6b**) which is very similar to the avoided crossing shown by the 6-point B-spline at $c = 18.3$ (Fig. 7.1). The close proximity of the two events is similar to the cubic Bézier results at $c = 3.6$, except that here we have an avoided crossing, not a Type 2 crossing. As well, the proximity of the events makes this situation numerically very challenging because the determinant of $\mathbf{M}$ is quite small over an extended range of the variable a_1. The variable β_1 (Fig. 10.5) shows the same qualitative behavior as a_1.

7. *S-shaped spline*. This item represents a localized disturbance that occurs at $1.2 < c < 5.1$ with $a_1 \approx 9$. On this branch, the two opposing Bézier arm lengths, a_1 and b_1, are sufficiently long that the spline curve is temporarily coerced into a

very sharp S-shaped bend, leading to a multiplicity of solutions. The location of the bend relative to the nearest $u(t_i)$ value is critical, so changing N, for example, would have a major affect on the feature, in the sense that it would be relocated to a different region of c, but would not disappear. Luckily this feature occurs only on a solution that has a very high rms error, so it is of no practical interest.

In summary, the Beta1-spline has a number of unique numerical challenges that make it difficult to work with. These are related to the fact that the asymmetric degree of freedom appears to allow for a lot of lateral movement of arm lengths without affecting the rms error very much. For example, the compound events seen in Case 6 represent a serious disturbance in the variables a_1, a_2, and β_1, but they are not even observable in the rms error in Fig. 10.4. However, apart from the numerical difficulties, the Beta1-spline has one significant advantage, namely that it can assist in providing a smooth transition from symmetric behavior to asymmetric behavior.

Chapter 11
Conclusions

The Least Squares Orthogonal Distance Fitting method (ODF) can be represented as two nested sub-problems. The inner problem is the minimization of the distance from a point on the curve to be fit to the spline curve we are using to perform the fit. The outer problem is the minimization of the error functional with respect to changes in the parameters of the spline, subject to this constraint of minimized distance. The equations to be solved represent the first-order response of the error functional to change, while the rate of convergence is governed by the second-order response. The solution can be characterized as being either a local minimum or a single or double saddle point by inspecting the number of negative eigenvalues the second order response matrix contains. The response matrix contains three types of contributions. There are terms proportional to the first order (Jacobian) response of the residual error function, which will be present even if the spline curve is a linear function of its parameters. There are other terms proportional to the second-order (Hessian) response matrix which will be present only if there are non-linear effects due to internal constraints between different fitting parameters. These will occur only when using Beta-splines for the curve fit. Finally there are terms caused by the simultaneous response of the solution for the inner distance minimization to changes in the fitting parameters in the outer loop. These terms are unique to the ODF method and play a crucial role in determining the rate of convergence of the algorithm.

When applied to the problem of fitting a family of shapes which are capable of changing from a symmetric to a highly asymmetric form, the solutions to the ODF problem often consist of a rather complex set of solutions, some of which are more appropriate in the symmetric case while others behave better in the asymmetric limit. These solutions often coalesce and disappear in pairs as the shape of the function to be fit changes. In each case these merges are associated with a zero of an eigenvalue in the response matrix, such that one of the branches is a local minimum and the other branch is a single saddle point, which merge as the corresponding eigenvalues approach each other at zero; or, alternatively, a single saddle point can merge with a double saddle point. In addition to these merges, it is also possible for two solutions to cross each other and interchange character from being a minimum to a saddle point and vice-versa. These crossovers can be identified by the fact that the response matrix $\mathbf{M}$ and the augmented matrix $\mathbf{M}^+$ both have zero eigenvalues at the crossover.

The solution set always has the property that it is possible to maintain continuity of the rms error while continuously navigating the entire family of shapes, but the individual shape parameters of the spline will normally change discontinuously when switching between different branches. Improving the sophistication of the splines we are using in the fit by adding additional degrees of freedom may improve the quality of the fit but does not in any way mitigate the size or severity of the discontinuities that occur in the fitting parameters.

The results of applying this method to a family of hypoTrochoid shapes using six different splines are summarized in Fig. 11.1. The splines range from a cubic Bézier with 2 degrees of freedom (d.f.) to a quartic Bézier with 4 d.f., to a series of uniform cubic B-splines and Beta-splines with anywhere from 4 to 6 d.f. In each case we have plotted only the optimum rms error, showing only the best branch at any time. The quartic Bézier is clearly the best overall solution, which is particularly impressive since it only has 4 d.f. while other splines have as many as 6 d.f. However, this is of little practical value since this type of curve is not supported by standard computer graphics libraries for rendering curves. The cubic splines all show two features in common, namely a maximum error in the asymmetric region (large c) and a minimum error in the symmetric region where c is smaller but not zero. Rather surprisingly, none of the splines show a global minimum error at exactly $c = 0$, except for the Beta2-spline, which is characterized by an adjustable symmetric node at the intermediate breakpoint. The 5-point and 6-point uniform B-splines represent perhaps the simplest way of improving the fit since they

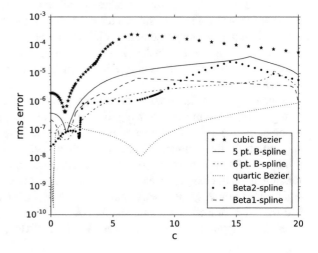

Fig. 11.1 Summary of rms error for six splines

both retain the linearity of the spline function so they are very easy to implement. However, they do not change the overall qualitative behavior of the original cubic Bézier result in any particular way; specifically, they both have a rather nasty discontinuity in arm lengths as one makes the switch from an asymmetric limit to a symmetric limit around $c = 16$ or 18, respectively. In specialized cases the two Beta-splines can be very useful. The Beta2-spline makes excellent use of only one additional d.f., relative to the 5-point B-spline, for the symmetric region where $c < 10$. It is the only spline that has a global minimum at $c = 0$. The Beta1-spline does a correspondingly good job in the asymmetric region where $c > 10$. The Beta1-spline is perhaps the most intriguing of all the methods since the new parameter it introduces is capable of adjusting the degree of asymmetry at the intermediate breakpoint, which leads to what is arguably the most consistent improvement over the 5-point B-spline for a large range of c. However, this comes with additional numerical complexity as well, when attempting to converge to a solution. In any event, before choosing one of the Beta-splines, it would first be necessary to consider the symmetry of the object being fit. If the object to be fit does not possess any clearly defined symmetry, then the uniform B-spline with multiple intermediate breakpoints may be the safest method of improving the result, since it is less complex than using the Beta-splines.

Printed in the United States
By Bookmasters